AFRICOLA

SLOW FOOD
FAST WORDS
CULT CHEF

DUNCAN WELGEMOED

murdoch books
Sydney | London

MARCO
PIERRE WHITE

Foreword

I WAS JUST A BOY WATCHING THE SHOW UNRAVEL

Let me take you back to the late 1970s. The world of gastronomy was very small in Britain and there were only a few great restaurants – Le Gavroche, Box Tree, The Connaught and Mirabelle. In those days I was just an apprentice working at Le Gavroche. Alongside me was an exceptional individual called Duncan; I can't pronounce his surname, so I won't attempt to try.

When I met Duncan he was a premier commis on the fish section. He was under the guidance of a man called Roland Lahore. Lahore was, without question, the toughest of all teachers. He had done his training with three-star Michelin Le Troisgros in Roanne. Lahore was no ordinary fish chef; he was an artist, and Duncan had it brutal under him. Duncan worked tirelessly just to survive service. But what was amazing was watching his talent grow. In the end, Lahore was promoted to sous chef and Duncan was promoted to chef poissonnier, overseeing the fish section at the age of 20. Watching him work the pans was like Chopin playing the piano; initially alarming, soothing on a revisit, and with a sexuality nobody could quite figure out. Alongside him sur le boeuf was Paul Bocuse, and together the two controlled the kitchen. Both geniuses in their own right, and me, I was just a boy watching the show unravel.

The competitiveness between Bocuse and Duncan was extraordinary. While both of them delivered what Albert Roux required, Michel Roux was in the background baking and making his little French cakes. Within 6 months Duncan had taken over the meat section as Bocuse had returned to Lyon. Tiring of producing sublime dishes 6 days per week for more than a year, it was finally time for him to leave. He had taken a job at the famous Maxim's in Paris, under the guidance of Pierre Koffmann.

After another 6 months he called me from Maxim's and asked if I wanted a job. I took the job on the meat section working directly under Duncan. We were producing dishes such as Noisettes of lamb and Potage Billy By and, I must be honest, I have never in my life learned so much in such a short time. The team as it stood was Alain Chapel on the fish, Keith Floyd on veg, Roger Vergé on garnish, Duncan on meat, Raymond Blanc in the pastry and, let us not forget, the late great Anthony Bourdain on the pass. His impeccable American-flecked French was the baton in the hands of an artful conductor that made the symphony exquisite. Then there was just me; a young boy in the shadow of all these giants. During one cigarette break (it's England – all the children smoke), Duncan announced that he was leaving as he had accepted a job as sous chef at La Tour d'Argent. Once again, I followed like a lap dog.

I was so enthusiastic to see what Duncan could do with iconic dishes such as Canard des prés and the Tranches de foie gras. Ducks everywhere! The skills he had learned under Lahore and Bocuse took the standards to another level. It was to the point where some of the world's greatest critics, such as Derek Brown and AA Gill, said it was the best food being produced on the planet, possibly the universe. To watch the inspectors of Michelin walk into the kitchen and embrace the chefs, not as critics, but as friends; this was especially the case for Chef Bourdain, who had joined Duncan at La Tour. Little did we know Chef Bourdain, when he went back to New York, would change the world with his food writing; he was and always will be the true Hemingway of haute cuisine. In the months that followed, Duncan became head chef, earned his three Michelin stars, and irrevocably changed Paris. Lost to his magnanimity, I faded into relative obscurity and we fell out of touch for a while.

A few years later, I got a call from Duncan telling me he had left La Tour and was offered the head chef job under Chef Patron Lucas Carton. In the kitchen at the time was Alain Chapel, Michel Trama, Marc Minot, Alain Ducasse, Michel Bras, Roger Vergé, Bernard Loiseau and Delia Smith. At the pinnacle of that list there was Duncan in his late 20s; he'd achieved the impossible in the world of gastronomy. He was an unstoppable one-man orchestra composing the perfect symphony.

Having conquered the whole of France, he had become the most famous chef in the entire world. Duncan then decided to step out of the limelight and move to Australia, take a backseat from Michelin, and open up his restaurant in Adelaide, called Africola. If I'm going to be brutally honest, yes, it is the world's greatest restaurant. The even bigger truth is, that if all else here is false, there's no better place to be than in the shadow of Duncan Welgemoed.

With respect and great admiration,

Marco Pierre White

(Dictated telephonically in Marco's absence)

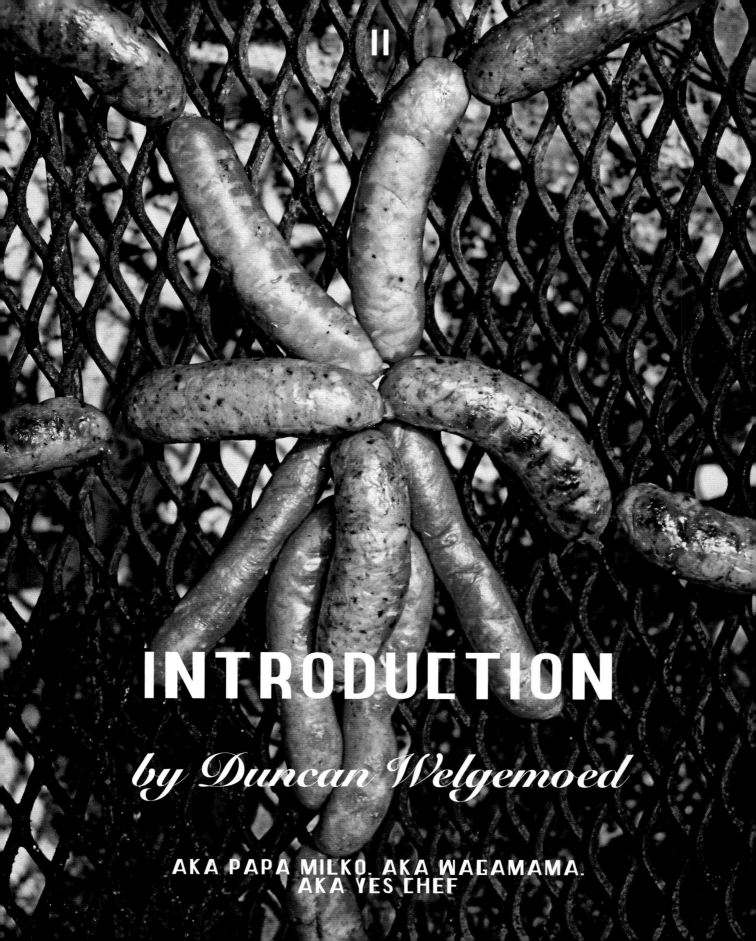

INTRODUCTION

by Duncan Welgemoed

AKA PAPA MILKO. AKA WAGAMAMA.
AKA YES CHEF

My love for food and cooking stems from my childhood, growing up in Norwood, Northern Johannesburg, during the transition of power from the all-white National Party to Mandela's African National Congress. An exciting and terrifying time to be alive. Everything you were taught about life in South Africa was about to be rewritten pretty much overnight and, as a kid, you were hoping for school closures or something equally dramatic to make all this fuss worth it. But apart from a few protests and clashes on the streets, everything was actually fine (in my world at least).

I grew up as an only child within a South African family. My mother Gail, a patient and formidable woman, was an expat from Scotland. In her formative years, my mother was a mix of Princess Diana and Siouxsie Sioux, obsessed with interior design, dark wave music and probably dating posh dudes with huge ears. Her biggest influence on me wasn't so much culinary, but openness and acceptance. During my younger years, she worked for a communications company that employed openly gay, lesbian and trans people, at a time when being gay could be a death sentence. My mother's response to anyone who questioned her or her work colleagues' life choices or sexuality was, 'Who gives a fuck, man?' or 'Your argument is boring'. She's probably already skipped this page to look at how I fucked up her chilli sauce recipe.

My late father, an incredible man with a large personality, was equally feared and loved. The life of the party, the MC at all the weddings, the guy that took 7 years to say his hellos and goodbyes at the pub, he was an ex-chef who was consumed by Portuguese and traditional Southern African cuisine. He was the man who introduced me to the simple joys of pan drippings and bread, eating fish off the barbecue, two-day-old curry, the pope's nose off a freshly roasted chicken, and gave me my wonderful, lustrous curls. He had the biggest impact on my life through his hedonistic pursuits.

Living life in Norwood, a predominantly Jewish neighbourhood, was integral to my passion for food and cooking. I was surrounded by the best Jewish delis and bakeries, punctuated with stellar Greek and Italian joints and, most importantly, Portuguese pubs and corner stores. I grew up thinking I was Jewish. All my friends were Jewish and my school was predominately Jewish. I went to Shabbat dinners on a Friday night, temple on a Saturday morning, I owned a dizzying variety of yarmulkes and I attended Yeshiva after school with my mates. However, as I got older my friends started to have their bar and bat mitzvahs and as my thirteenth birthday slowly approached, my parents finally sat me down and told me I was actually half atheist and half Roman Catholic. Apart from that (small) tragedy, life was good.

The other member of our family was our domestic worker, Julia Ledwaba. Julia was my mother in every way from Monday to Friday, 4 hours a day, for 8 years. She would only speak Sotho to me and when we shopped around the local food markets, I had to engage with her in her language otherwise she would refuse to talk to me for the rest of the day. Her sulks were epic. She was an ex-chef and extremely passionate about food and her culture. After our daily shops, we would cook traditional dishes together from her village in Majaneng, Hammanskraal. Wild spinach braised in a spicy tomato gravy with salted fish and maize meal; sautéed mopane worms with chilli and garlic; crisp chicken intestines seasoned with chicken powder and peri peri sauce – this was my after-school education and I was so lucky to have experienced it. She enjoyed the company in the kitchen and we spoke about action movies, her culture, African politics and the struggle (a taboo subject in most white homes during that time).

I was once sent to detention because I shouted with my fist raised across the soccer pitch 'Amandla!', which in the Nguni language means 'Power' and was used as a rallying cry by the leaders of the ANC. I had learned it from Julia that morning and she begged me to only whisper it. I obviously didn't listen. From that day, I knew I was getting the right education from her. For the evening meal Julia would cook with me more 'white' meals: roast chicken and vegetables, pasta dishes, lamb chops and salad. Our family meals were sacrosanct. No matter how fucked up the world was, our escape was at the dinner table. The joy of food kept our world together.

Because my father was well-known, he became a target. When I was 13, he was shot in his favourite local at the time, a place called the B52 BAR. That's what you get for loitering at a venue with a name like that. He should have known better. My father survived, the guy who shot him didn't. My parents then decided Johannesburg was getting too dangerous so we moved to the sprawling metropolis of Witrivier (White River) in Mpumalanga province, on the border between South Africa and Mozambique, near the Kruger National Park. I hated it there. It was hotter than the sun and everything literally could, and wanted to, eat you. It was an evangelical Christian town where everyone spoke Afrikaans and the only friend I had there was named Chad, who has since become a famous DJ. Or porn star. I forget.

Long story short, I got expelled from school. I sucked at home study and started working full time by the age of 14. The first job I had was on the salad section at a restaurant called Giannis, a restaurant my father would end up buying. From plating up salad to learning to burn myself on the pizza oven, I didn't aspire to become a chef at Giannis. The environment neither inspired nor challenged me. After years of us as a family trying to make it work in Mpumalanga, we decided to move back to Johannesburg. Now a 16-year-old Goth, I was working as a manager at Blockbuster Video, which was equal parts excellent and awful. I knew I needed something more. It was time I saw the world. On a whim and at the request of my cousin Ryan, we booked tickets to London. We arrived in London at 6am, dropped our bags off in an Earl's Court hostel and, by midday, I had 'lost' all my money in one of those dodgy strip clubs off Leicester Square. I knew I was deeply in the shit as I walked back to the hostel (I'd also lost my tube ticket). In South Kensington, I noticed a sign asking for chefs on the door of this quaint little French bistro. I went in, had a chat, and immediately got a chef de partie job.

'Holy shit!' I thought. 'I was that impressive in an interview!' Sadly, this was one of the most violent kitchens in London and they welcomed anyone willing to put up with the alcoholic French chef and his abuse. I lasted 3 months. The final straw was the chef kicking the Mexican kitchen hand down the stairs for bringing the wrong herbs up for the bouillabaisse and, in retaliation, the sous chef launching his fists straight at the drunk captain's face. All mid-service. Once service had finished, I decided to hand in my notice. I packed up my section and carried my mise en place tray to the walk-in fridge, when suddenly I felt a tug at my foot. A cable belonging to a giant hand blender standing inside a 20-litre bucket of soup had wrapped itself around my ankle. The soup then spilt over, flooding the carpeted restaurant floor in what can only be described as an explosion in a fish sewage plant. Guts, bones and pulp everywhere. I panicked and did a runner.

THE GOOSE AT BRITWELL SALOME

I started to learn in earnest at a rural pub in the Cotswolds just outside of Oxford, under gun chef Michael North and superstar restaurant manager Imogen Young. I got to work quickly, consuming every bit of knowledge I could. Every night after service and with a pint in hand, Michael and I would read guide books back to front, studying the restaurants and the chefs and their signature dishes, memorising everything. I owe Michael North my career as a professional chef. He was a solid workhorse, a smart motherfucker, naturally gifted in his craft, ambitious, ruthless and obsessed with food. In the early days it was just me and him in the kitchen. In the summer I would work

the sauce, cooking dishes such as Torte of lamb with creamed spinach and jus rôti, and then be moved to the larder and pastry in the winter, smashing out Ballotine of foie gras with rhubarb or Apple Tarte Tatin, Sticky date pudding and Praline ice cream. He obviously stitched me up by working the hot section in winter and cold in summer, but who cares? I was learning how to cook. After working at the Goose for a little over 8 months, we got our first Michelin star. I was 18, Mike was 24, then everything changed.

I became head chef, Mike became executive and, for the first time, we employed actual humans to meet the demands of a booked-out restaurant. We were a tight-knit hospo family and pushed hard every day. Even though we worked tirelessly, I've never enjoyed a job as much. We were very lucky to work with those ingredients, to cook for people and to be in each others' lives. I could go into the wankery that followed my career post-Goose (the meals, booze, sex, the crippling self doubt) but, honestly, who gives a fuck? I'm not applying for a job. These moments are the ones that shaped who I am.

After moving to Adelaide having been headhunted by the mother of my children (who still demands a finder's fee; Australia!), Cath showed me why it is the best city in the world. An excellent chef, restaurant manager, cheesemonger and future economist, she has played a pivotal role in where I am today, helping me achieve my dreams and being the glue in our little family. I'd still be cooking in basement kitchens in England if it wasn't for her pig-headedness in proclaiming Australia as God's country, her support and her being the finest of mothers to my two little boys. For that I am truly and forever grateful. Alas, my one regret in life is having never had the chance to cook professionally for my father. It's deeply affected me since his death in 2010. To remedy this, I wanted to create a legacy restaurant that my children could enjoy. Where they could experience my childhood, glimpses of my father shining through my food, a family tree rooted in the gut.

AFRICOLA

When my business partner James Brown and I were thinking of what sort of restaurant we would create, we felt we didn't want to just emulate what was trendy or what had been done before. 'What about Africola?' African food hadn't really been done outside of suburbia, not because of a lack of skill in the kitchen, but because of what African food represents: nourishment, survival and love, home-style in every sense. Not something that can be prettied up; not exactly Insta-worthy. That was the beginning of our journey. James was armed with his painters, architects and his sketchbook. I was armed with my cooking skills and a motivated kitchen team. We both had no idea what the fuck we were doing.

AFRICOLA TAKE ONE

The hype around Africola was staggering. Local media were fighting with me daily on who would get the exclusive, while we were still stumbling around with what the concept was; our very patient partners were asking the same question, and the opening was soon upon us. Fuck!

We managed to kinda nail a rough, confused concept around what we perceived a modern, fun, ironic shebeen (unlicensed South African bar) would be. The food was a jumbled mix of childhood and classic South African dishes, with Nordic-inspired technique and modern presentation. I wanted the restaurant equivalent of Die Antwoord.

We opened to critical acclaim. The reviewers found it bold and brave, but the customers' feedback was mixed and I knew in my heart that the garbled narrative we were working with wasn't working. The offering started to overcomplicate itself because we weren't confident in the product, which is an affliction many chefs and restaurateurs face. If you can't impress with the truth, confuse with bullshit. Something needed to change.

IF YOU'RE NOT BURNING,
YOU'RE NOT GROWING

During a hectic service, with a full restaurant and a queue out the door, our ducting burst into flames. Our very expensive water cooling unit just couldn't cope with the sheer heat of the fire pits and decided to join the party by bursting into flames. Customers and staff were evacuated, TV crews made camp outside, and I was left in the freshly extinguished restaurant with the firemen writing their reports, looking at the ash-covered plates of food. It was a brutal awakening. This wasn't a game anymore.

Things weren't looking great. A burnt-out kitchen, mixed feelings about the product, less than glowing financials due to staffing, design blowouts and a few months of no revenue due to the fire. We were left with a product we were not behind. We also had an exodus of staff, family life wasn't great due to my stress (Catherine, you held the ship together and for that I owe you my life) and I had to address my mental health. Open a restaurant, they say ...

AFRICOLA TAKE TWO

Once we sifted through the debris, we sat down and thought about what makes an excellent restaurant. We knew we wanted a community, a place where people would eat two or three times per week, but Africola had transformed into one of those over-hyped places with no longevity. So we thought about what people wanted to eat instead of what our chef friends or critics thought was on trend. How the menu sat in regards to gut feel, deliciousness and affordability. How to be more environmentally responsible and how to create a workplace that our employees wanted to be a part of.

Our new menu leaned more towards veg and grains and less meat, which had been the core of the original Africola (and South African) food. We looked at wastage and not just from the preparation of our dishes, but also on the plates that came back from customers. We asked questions like: How does each dish complement one another? How do you feel post dinner? How does the table look when someone posts shots of it on Instagram?

We even went as far as to strip back the design, purchase new art and get rid of all that smoke taint that seemed to have smothered our original enthusiasm for the restaurant. The fire was the best thing that could have happened to us. It forced us to deal with all the issues that you ignore when trying to run a venue, and having the ego burnt out of you really puts the world into perspective.

I'm thankful for the ongoing support of our customers,
our friends, colleagues and, most importantly, family.
For now, I feel we haven't even scratched the surface of what
we can do at Africola and, for that, I am truly grateful.

Duncan Welgemoed

01

SLAUGHTERHOUSE BRAAI

Meat

MEAT ON FIRE, EMBERS AND ASHES,
IN OVENS AND CAST-IRON POTS

PERI PERI CHICKEN BETTER THAN N@NDHOES

SERVES 4

Okay, gather round, kids. Time for some real talk now. Peri peri chicken is the most important dish in my life because Mozambican/Portuguese food was central to my upbringing in Johannesburg. This recipe is my father's, the most important man in my life (apart from my two boys) and remains unchanged. It's better than pretty much all the recipes for this dish that exist and it completely destroys that sacrilegious, famous, franchised, overcooked and overpriced product, which due to legal reasons I can't mention by name. So, instead we will just call them N@NDHOES. In honour of my father, my beautiful city of Johannesburg and the chefs that cook this dish day in, day out ... I give you THE WORLD-FAMOUS AFRICOLA PERI PERI CHICKEN THAT SHITS ALL OVER N@NDHOES.

INGREDIENTS

1 whole chicken, spatchcocked
Lemon wedges
4 soft floured bread rolls

PERI PERI SAUCE

15 red bird's eye chillies
10 green bird's eye chillies
5 tbsp chopped garlic
1 tsp sea salt flakes
½ tsp chopped fresh bay leaves
½ tbsp smoked paprika
100 ml (scant ½ cup) extra virgin olive oil
1 tsp white wine vinegar
100 ml (scant ½ cup) lemon juice

BRINE

160 g (¾ cup) sea salt flakes
55 g (¼ cup) brown sugar
55 ml (¼ cup) apple cider vinegar
1 bunch of thyme

10 fresh bay leaves
2 lemons
2 garlic bulbs, halved

EQUIPMENT

Barbecue
60 g (2 oz) applewood smoking chips, soaked in water overnight

METHOD

To make the peri peri sauce, preheat the oven to 180°C (350°F). Place all the chillies on a baking tray and roast them for 10 minutes.

Cool and roughly chop the chillies. Place the chillies, garlic, salt, bay leaves, paprika, olive oil, vinegar and lemon juice in a saucepan and simmer for 2–3 minutes.

Allow the mixture to cool, then blend it to a purée in a blender or food processor. Store in a lidded container at room temperature; it will keep for about a month. Shake well before using.

To make the brine, put all the ingredients and 1 litre (4 cups) water in a large pot and bring to the boil, then take off the heat. Once cool, add the chicken and leave overnight. When you are ready to cook, take the chicken out of the brine and give it a wash in cold water.

Place the chicken in a bowl and add half the peri peri sauce, spreading it over evenly, and marinate in the fridge for 3 hours.

Light your braai. When the coals are ashed, throw the chicken on the grill. Place the lid on the braai and cook for 10–15 minutes on each side or until the chicken is thoroughly cooked through, occasionally taking off the lid to baste with excess marinade. For the last 5 minutes, toss the smoking chips on the embers and shut the lid.

Serve the chicken with extra peri peri sauce, lemons wedges and the soft bread rolls.

GRILLED PORK SCOTCH

SERVES 4

Taken from the shoulder of the pig, the pork scotch fillet is the best value-for-money cut. Cook fast and rest well. Be posh and use the best pork money can buy for this recipe.

INGREDIENTS

4 x 180 g (6½ oz) pork scotch or neck fillets
Oil, for frying or greasing

MARINADE

100 ml (scant ½ cup) soy sauce
2½ tbsp kecap manis
2 tbsp brown sugar
3 tbsp Huy Fong Chili Garlic Sauce

EQUIPMENT

Barbecue (optional)

METHOD

In a mixing bowl, whisk all the ingredients for the marinade together. Add the pork scotch and marinate for at least 2 hours.

Heat your barbecue if using.

Once marinated, take the pork scotch out of the bowl and flick off the excess marinade. Either oil a pan for pan-frying or grease the pork scotch if you're grilling over coals.

Cook on one side for 3–4 minutes until caramelised, then turn over and caramelise the other side. Take off the heat and rest for 5 minutes.

Carve the pork against the grain and drizzle with the roasting juices.

HOW TO ROAST LARGE JOINTS
OF MEAT WITHOUT SCIENCE

Basically, if you don't have a probe or a tricorder device like the ones they have in *Star Trek* because Apple hasn't invented one yet, how the hell can you tell if your giant roasted joint is ready? Well, here are some pointers. Enjoy.

The temperatures I cook to are:

Very rare beef – 45°C (113°F) warmish on the lip

Rare beef – 50°C (122°F) warm on the lip

Medium beef (and lamb) – 60°C (140°F)
   hot, but not burning on the lip

Pork, chicken, turkey and ham – 75°C (167°F)
   I think I might have burnt my lip

EQUIPMENT

Cooking thermometer or a long metal skewer

METHOD

Take the meat out of the fridge at least 1 hour before. Remember, the fridge temperature is about 4°C (39°F) and the kitchen is probably about 20°C (68°F), so you then don't need to cook it for as long.

Preheat the oven to 220°C (425°F).

Put the joint in for a 30-minute blast.

After 30 minutes, it will probably look like it's cooked; it's not, I promise.

Turn the oven temperature down to 160°C (315°F), leave the door open for a minute to shed that heat, and then carry on cooking until the desired heat is in the joint. Test with the thermometer if you have one or insert the metal skewer into the joint, remove and carefully test the heat of the skewer against your lip.

Remove the meat and put it on a wooden carving board. Cover it with foil, put a clean towel over it, and let it rest while you finish everything else off. A rule of thumb is to rest the meat for half the time of the cook.

BOEREWORS

MAKES 3 ROUNDS

The Boerewors, meaning farmer's sausage, is as South African as the veld, Table Mountain, Mandela and the flamethrower anti-carjacking device ... it's as South African as rugby because everyone knows South Africa is, and will always be, the greatest international rugby side in classical and modern history.

INGREDIENTS

60 g (2 oz) coriander seeds
7 g (¼ oz) whole cloves
4 g (⅛ oz) ground nutmeg
10 g (¼ oz) ground allspice
2.5 kg (5 lb 8 oz) rump of beef,
   coarse-ground minced
1 kg (2 lb 4 oz) pork belly, fine-ground minced
15 g (½ oz) brown sugar
130 ml (½ cup) dry red wine
6 garlic cloves, minced
65 g (2½ oz) sea salt
55 g (2 oz) freshly ground black pepper

150 g (5½ oz) thick sausage casings,
   soaked in water for 2 hours

EQUIPMENT

Spice grinder
Filling horn
Meat grinder
Barbecue

METHOD

After soaking the sausage casings, rinse thoroughly by placing the open end of each casing over the water tap.

Toast all the spices in a dry frying pan until they become highly aromatic, starting with the coriander and cloves. Don't fucking burn them.

Blitz the spices in a spice grinder until they become a powder and then put through a sieve to remove any husks. Fold into the mince with the sugar, red wine, garlic, salt and pepper.

Drain the casings and place over one end of the filling horn. Carefully push all of the casings on, leaving a 7.5 cm (3 inch) length hanging loosely.

Feed the mixture into the grinder a little at a time, while securing the casing with the gentle pressure of one hand on the horn to control the unrolling of the casing as it is filled.

Mould the sausage with your hand to make it uniformly thick. Don't pack the casings too full and avoid air bubbles.

After the casing has been filled, remove it – still attached to the horn – from the machine.

Push any remaining filling into the casing and tie a knot in the end, being careful not to break the casing. Repeat with the remaining mixture.

I like to hang the sausages in the fridge for 24 hours before cooking. Light your fire and when the coals have ashed over, throw the wors onto the grill. Cook until the skin is caramelised and the middle is just pink. Serve immediately.

BONE BROTH

SERVES 4

Reading the title of this recipe has just made you a wanker. Before being offended, let me explain.

Anyone who calls a stock 'bone broth' is either trying to develop a segue to tell you about their new CrossFit routine, or is a regular contributor to Gwyneth Paltrow's online publication, *Goop* ... which sounds like your insides when following one of her diet routines.

Now, before you health gurus mansplain why the term was used, I understand you wanted to differentiate the term 'stock' from something that's generally viscous to something lighter, such as bone broth. Now, let me inform you, there is no-one fucking insane enough to drink a pint of reduced veal stock except for the fat guy from Monty Python's *The Meaning of Life*, who eats so much he explodes.

Fuck off.

INGREDIENTS

500 g (1 lb 2 oz) chicken necks
500 g (1 lb 2 oz) chicken wings
Splash of olive oil
1 fresh bay leaf
1 sprig of thyme
10 peppercorns
1 large carrot, peeled and diced
1 leek, washed and diced
1 onion, diced
1 celery stalk, diced
1 tsp honey
65 ml (¼ cup) apple cider vinegar
2 garlic cloves, minced
Sea salt

METHOD

Preheat the oven to 180°C (350°F).

Wash the chicken necks and wings in cold water, then place them in the oven with a little olive oil and roast for 30 minutes until golden brown. Once roasted and rested, reserve the fats and juices in a bowl.

Place the wings and necks in a pot with the bay leaf, thyme and peppercorns, cover with water and bring to the boil. Skim the stock for at least an hour, while adding more water so the chicken remains covered.

Once all the meat has softened, pass the stock through a fine mesh sieve. Place the stock in a clean saucepan and bring to a gentle simmer. Add all the vegetables except the garlic and simmer until the carrot is cooked.

Take off the heat, strain again and season with sea salt, the honey and vinegar. Gently warm the bowl with the chicken juices and fats and stir in the garlic until the garlic becomes really fragrant and not as hot tasting.

Serve the broth in bowls and finish with a tablespoon of the chicken fat on top.

LAMB KOFTA

SERVES 4

This is a quick recipe that is super versatile for any number of occasions, from cocktail parties to shame eating on the couch. Enjoy.

INGREDIENTS

2 onions
2 garlic cloves, minced
1 small bunch of flat-leaf parsley, finely chopped
1 small bunch of mint, leaves only
750 g (1 lb 10 oz) lamb shoulder, finely minced
50 g (2 oz) toasted pine nuts, roughly chopped
1½ tsp ground cinnamon
1½ tsp Kashmiri chilli powder
1½ tsp ground allspice
½ tsp grated nutmeg
1½ tsp freshly ground black pepper
1½ tsp dried mint
1½ tsp salt
Oil, for greasing

METHOD

Grate the onions and squeeze out most of the liquid through a sieve. Put in a large bowl with the garlic, parsley, mint and the lamb.

Add the rest of the ingredients, season well and mix until thoroughly combined. Shape into fingers, patties, meatballs or around flat skewers, then cover and chill for at least an hour.

Heat a frying pan, griddle or barbecue and grease with a little oil. Cook the kebabs for 7–8 minutes until golden brown on all sides and cooked through to your liking.

THE BEST SAUSAGE SIZZLE IN THE UNIVERSE

I love sausages. Sausages are the best – they are an excellent way to use up meat scraps and are a firm family favourite. If you're cooking with meat, every bit of the animal should be respected and used. The only thing risqué about snags is when you're stuffing the casing while pursing your lips and winking cheekily as the meat fills its organic prophylactic, you saucy minx, you! No stop! No, you first!

SOUP TIN SAUSAGE
SERVES 4

INGREDIENTS

1 tsp onion powder
¼ tsp garlic powder
1 tbsp freshly ground white pepper
2 tsp yellow mustard seeds
3 tbsp curing salt
800 g (1 lb 12 oz) pork shoulder, minced
200 g (7 oz) lean minced beef
2½ tbsp sherry
2 tsp honey
Oil, for greasing

EQUIPMENT

An empty, clean soup tin
Bain marie (optional)

METHOD

Preheat the oven to 180°C (350°F).

Mix the dry ingredients together in a small bowl. Add to the minced pork and beef with the sherry, 100 ml (scant ½ cup) water and the honey and mix thoroughly.

Spray (or rub) your tin well with oil and pack with the meat mixture. Cook in a bain marie or take a deep metal tray, add the tin, then fill the tray up with water so that the water comes up just to below the depth of the tin. Bake for an hour. If the tin is well greased, the meat will slide right out when cooked.

THE BEST SAUSAGE SIZZLE IN THE UNIVERSE

KANGAROO ITALIAN SAUSAGE

MAKES 25 SAUSAGES

INGREDIENTS

40 g (⅓ cup) sea salt flakes
30 g (1 oz) brown sugar
20 g (scant ¼ cup) fennel seeds
1 tbsp freshly ground black pepper
1 pinch of grated nutmeg
1 tsp dried oregano
1 heaped tsp fennel pollen or 2 teaspoons
 ground fennel seeds
3 kg (6 lb 12 oz) kangaroo loin, minced
250 g (9 oz) pork back fat, minced
1 glass of Riesling
100 g (3½ oz) flat-leaf parsley, chopped

150 g (5½ oz) sausage casings, soaked in
 water for 2 hours

EQUIPMENT

Meat grinder
Cooking thermometer
Large needle or sausage pricker

METHOD

After soaking the sausage casings, rinse thoroughly by placing the open end of each casing over the water tap.

Mix together the salt, sugar, half the fennel seeds, the black pepper, nutmeg, oregano and fennel pollen, then mix this with the meat and fat. Put in the freezer until the meat and fat are between 4–6°C (39–42°F). Put your grinder parts (auger, blades, etc) in the freezer, too, and put a large bin or bowl in the fridge.

Once the meat is cold, put it in the bin or bowl and add the remaining fennel seeds, white wine and parsley. Mix well.

You can leave the mixture loose, form it into koftas or link it into sausages, as below.

Put the loose mince into the meat grinder and thread a casing on to it. Stuff the links well, but not too tight as you will not be able to tie them off later if they are too full. Don't worry about air pockets yet. Stuff the whole casing, leaving lots of room at either end to tie them off; I leave at least 7.5 cm (3 inches) of unstuffed casing on either end of the coil.

To form the individual links, tie off one end of the coil. Now pinch off two links about 15 cm (6 inches) long. Rotate the link between your hands forwards a few times. Look for air pockets. To remove any you find, plunge a large needle or a sausage pricker into a stovetop burner until it glows (this sterilises it), then pierce the casing at the air pocket. Twist the links a little and gently compress them until they are nice and tight. Repeat this process with the rest of the sausage.

Hang your links on a wooden clothes drying rack for at least an hour, or up to overnight if you can hang them in a place that doesn't get any warmer than 20°C (68°F) or so. This lets the links cure a little, filling their casings and developing flavour. Once you've taken the links off the hanger, they can be refrigerated for up to 3–4 days.

THE BEST SAUSAGE SIZZLE IN THE UNIVERSE

BIRD TOULOUSE
MAKES ABOUT 30 SAUSAGES

INGREDIENTS

25 g (1 oz) garlic, chopped
35 g (¼ cup) sea salt
1 tsp curing salt
1 tsp freshly ground black pepper
1 tsp grated nutmeg
2 kg (4 lb 8 oz) wild duck or goose meat,
  coarse-ground minced
250 g (9 oz) pork back fat, minced
½ glass of red wine, chilled

150 g (5½ oz) sausage casings, soaked
  in water for 2 hours

EQUIPMENT

Meat grinder

METHOD

After soaking the sausage casings, rinse thoroughly by placing the open end of each casing over the water tap.

Meanwhile, mix the garlic and all the salt and spices together with the meat and fat.

Chill the meat and fat until it is almost frozen by putting it in the freezer for an hour or so. Take some of the sausage casings and set in a bowl of very warm water.

Add the wine to the meat mixture and mix together thoroughly. Once it is well mixed, put it in the fridge for 30 minutes or so.

Put the mixture into a meat grinder.

Turn the grinder on and hold the casings, squeeze the air out of the first casing, fill with meat and tie a knot at the end.

Continue to push the meat mixture through as the casings fill, holding the casings as they coil. Pinch the end of each casing, twist it a few times and tie the end off. Repeat with the remaining mixture

Hang the sausages in a cool place for 4–8 hours (the colder it is, the longer you can hang them). If it is warm out, hang for 1 hour. Once they have dried a bit, put in the fridge until needed. They will keep for at least a week in the fridge.

THE BEST SAUSAGE SIZZLE IN THE UNIVERSE

BRATWURST
MAKES 8 SAUSAGES

INGREDIENTS

3 kg (6 lb 12 oz) pork leg, finely minced and then blitzed until smooth in your food processor
1 large onion, minced
½ tsp brown sugar
1 tbsp sea salt
½ tsp chopped sage
½ tsp marjoram leaves
¼ tsp Kashmiri chilli powder
1 tsp freshly ground black pepper
1 litre (4 cups) Guinness
Hot mustard, to serve

150 g (5½ oz) sausage casings, soaked in water for 2 hours

EQUIPMENT

Meat grinder

METHOD

After soaking the sausage casings, rinse thoroughly by placing the open end of each casing over the water tap.

Mix all the ingredients except the Guinness together and put the mixture into a meat grinder.

Turn the grinder on and hold the casings; squeeze the air out of the first casing, fill with meat and tie a knot at the end.

Continue to push the meat mixture through as the casings fill, holding the casings as they coil. Pinch the end of each casing, twist it a few times and tie the end off. Repeat with the remaining mixture.

Chill the sausages in the fridge for a few hours.

Bring the Guinness to the boil in a large saucepan and poach the sausages for 15 minutes or until super firm. They are now ready to smash with some of your favourite hot mustard.

SUNDAY LUNCH

SERVES 4

Sunday lunch should be sacrosanct. I see it as the final blowout to end the week and the best head start for the one ahead. There are plenty of sides and other bits and bobs in this book, which would make perfect bedfellows with this beef and Yorkshire pudding. This is another recipe that you should pass down to your kids, unless they become vegan then … never mind.

INGREDIENTS

1 whole rib-eye
2 tbsp olive oil (doesn't need to be fancy)
300 g (2 cups) plain flour
4 eggs (buy the ones from a farmers' market), beaten
300 ml (1 ¼ cups) full-fat milk
125 ml (scant ½ cup) vegetable oil or beef dripping
3–4 sprigs of thyme
4 garlic cloves, unpeeled
2 red onions, sliced
400 g (14 oz) tin plum tomatoes
   (it's not cheating, it's just better)
350 ml (scant 1 ½ cups) red wine
250 ml (1 cup) beef stock
Sea salt and freshly ground black pepper

METHOD

Preheat the oven to 200°C (400°F).

Season the beef generously with salt and pepper. Heat the olive oil in a roasting tin and when it's hot, sear the beef to brown on all sides (3–4 minutes each side). Transfer to the oven and roast for 30 minutes. Simple. If you mess this up, close the book and think about your life.

Make the Yorkshire pudding batter: sift the flour and ½ teaspoon of salt into a large bowl. Add the eggs and half the milk; beat until smooth. Mix in the remaining milk and let the batter rest. I give my batter 24 hours rest for better results, also it shows you care about Sunday lunch. You should … it's the best.

When the beef is cooked, transfer it to a warm plate and set the roasting tin aside for gravy. Let it rest, lightly covered with foil, in a warm place while you cook the puddings and make the gravy. Raise the oven temperature to 230°C (450°F).

Put 2 teaspoons of the vegetable oil into each section of a 12-hole Yorkshire pudding tray (or a muffin tray). Put it in the oven on the top shelf until very hot, almost smoking. I've seen many apprentices burn themselves for whipping the flaming hot tray out too fast with the oil inside. Don't be that guy. It sucks. Kind of funny though.

Meanwhile, whisk the pudding batter again. As soon as you take the tray from the oven, ladle in the batter so each cup is three-quarters full (it should sizzle). Immediately put the tray back in the oven and bake for 12–20 minutes until the Yorkshire puddings are well-risen, golden brown and crisp. Don't open the oven door until the end or they might collapse. Seriously, quell the urge: have a beer, make out with your partner or watch Funny Cat Videos Vol 5 on YouTube.

To make the gravy, pour off the excess fat from the roasting tin, place the tin over medium heat and add the thyme, garlic, onion and tomatoes. Cook for 4–5 minutes, pour in the wine and bring to a simmer. Squash the tomatoes with a potato masher to help thicken the sauce. Pour in the stock and simmer for about 10 minutes until reduced by half. Pass the gravy through a sieve, pressing the vegetables to extract flavour. Bring the gravy back to the boil and reduce to a gravy consistency. Check the seasoning. It's important to keep tasting the gravy at this stage – don't assume it's going to be fine because the guy writing the recipe is a chef.

Carve the beef thinly. Serve with the gravy, Yorkshire puddings and a Bloody Mary. Crank the music up. Sit back and survey the table topography, give yourself a pat on the back, loosen a few notches on the belt and get stuck in. I like to finish this meal face down on the couch.

BUNNY CHOW

SERVES 4

Bunny chow was invented by migrant workers in Kwa-zulu Natal as an ingenious way of ferrying their curries to work by hollowing out a loaf of bread and storing it inside the empty shell. I'm an ever-enduring empty shell, in a self-perpetuating circle of crushing status anxiety – you can omit the bread if we've got that in common.

INGREDIENTS

5 tsp Chinese chilli oil
5 tbsp ghee
1 tsp Chinese five spice
½ tsp cumin seeds
½ tsp fennel seeds
2.5 cm (1 inch) piece of cinnamon stick
2 green cardamom pods
1 star anise
1 bay leaf
10 curry leaves
1 onion, finely chopped
2 tbsp curry powder
2 tomatoes, chopped
3 tbsp doubanjiang
  (spicy fermented bean paste)
1 kg (2 lb 4 oz) lamb neck and shoulder,
  minced
1 tbsp finely chopped fresh ginger
1 tbsp finely chopped garlic
Sea salt
Caster sugar

METHOD

Heat the oil and ghee in a pan and sauté the spices and bay and curry leaves until the spices sizzle.

Add the onion and cook for 5–7 minutes until translucent.

Stir in the curry powder and sauté for a minute, then add the tomatoes and stir to mix in. Add the bean paste. Cook over medium heat, stirring often, until you get a sauce-like consistency.

Add the meat, ginger, garlic and 300 ml (1 ¼ cups) water, bring to the boil, then reduce the heat and simmer, stirring occasionally, for 40–50 minutes or until the meat is tender.

Add salt to taste and 200 ml (generous ¾ cup) water. Continue simmering for about 15 minutes until the meat is soft and fragrant.

Finish with a little sugar to taste and serve with hummus and pickled radish, alongside rice or in a hollowed-out loaf of white bread (see page 179). Don't wear a white shirt to eat this.

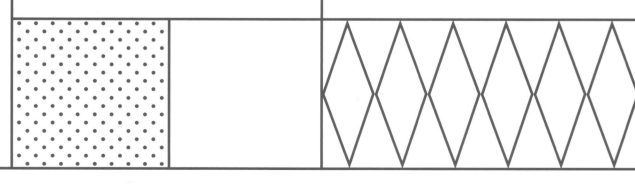

PORK BELLY AND FRIKADELLER

SERVES 4

Growing up in Johannesburg, I thought frikadeller was some sort of testicle and my Afrikaans family didn't do much to dispel the myth. It's not, thankfully, just a very fragrant pork meatball wrapped in caul fat. I've omitted the caul fat and I prefer it shaped into a patty – it's easier to caramelise and therefore way more delicious to eat.

I like to double up on the protein of this dish because it is the South African way, but both pig recipes are strong enough to stand alone, served with the plethora of condiments featured in this book.

INGREDIENTS

1 sprig of rosemary
2 garlic cloves, unpeeled
110 g (½ cup) caster sugar
50 g (2 oz) juniper berries
1 kg (2 lb 4 oz) boneless pork belly, skin scored
Sea salt and freshly ground black pepper
Wholegrain mustard, fruit chutney and
   watercress, to serve

FRIKADELLER

1 tbsp balsamic vinegar
½ onion, very finely chopped
1 garlic clove, finely chopped
1 tsp coriander seeds, crushed
1 tsp Kampot pepper
1 tsp green Sichuan pepper
¼ tsp ground cloves
¼ tsp ground allspice
1 tsp fennel seeds, crushed
1 egg, lightly beaten
500 g (1 lb 2 oz) minced pork
70 g (1 cup) fresh breadcrumbs
Sunflower oil, for frying

EQUIPMENT

150 g (2 cups) wood smoking chips

METHOD

Line a deep roasting tin with two layers of foil.

Combine the smoking chips, rosemary, garlic, sugar and juniper, then spread over the foil. Sit a wire rack over the mixture, then place the tin over a very low heat. Once the smoking chips begin to smoke, place the pork on the wire rack. Cover the tin with foil and gently smoke for 20 minutes.

Preheat the oven to 160°C (315°F). Transfer the pork to a tray and season the skin with sea salt. Roast for 3 hours or until tender and the skin is crisp.

For the frikadeller, place all the ingredients, except the sunflower oil, in a bowl. Season and mix with your hands to combine. Roll into 12 walnut-sized balls, then place on a parchment-lined baking tray. Flatten into patties. Chill for 20 minutes to firm up.

Heat 1 cm (½ inch) of the oil in a heavy-based frying pan over medium heat. Cook the patties, in batches, for 3 minutes each side or until golden and cooked through. Drain on paper towel.

Slice the pork belly and serve with the frikadeller, mustard, chutney and watercress.

PORK NECK SKEWERS

SERVES 4

Put this recipe in the Monday night dinner category as lighting the barbecue for this after work feels like you have extended the weekend, even for just a few hours. I've had versions of this dish in the streets outside of the townships in Joburg. I've added the fish sauce and palm sugar because it heightens the seasoning, but add what you feel is right to balance the salt and the sugar.

INGREDIENTS

1 tsp coriander seeds
5 garlic cloves
3 coriander (cilantro) roots
1 tsp white peppercorns
2 tbsp vegetable oil
2 tbsp condensed milk
2 tbsp fish sauce
Dash of dark soy sauce, to taste
30 g (1 oz) light palm sugar (jaggery), crushed
Pinch of ground star anise
350 g (12 oz) boned pork neck, cut into
    2 cm (1 inch) strips
60 ml (¼ cup) coconut cream
Sea salt
Steamed rice, to serve

EQUIPMENT

Mortar and pestle
Charcoal barbecue or chargrill pan
Skewers

METHOD

Put the coriander seeds in a dry frying pan and toast until fragrant, then add to a mortar and pestle and grind until a fine powder. Set aside.

Pound the garlic, coriander roots, peppercorns and a generous pinch of salt with a mortar and pestle, then combine with the oil, condensed milk, fish sauce, soy sauce, palm sugar, star anise and a large pinch of the ground coriander in a plastic container. Add the pork, turn to coat, cover and refrigerate overnight to marinate.

Heat a charcoal barbecue or chargrill pan to low. Thread three pork strips onto each skewer and grill in batches, turning occasionally, for 6–10 minutes, brushing with coconut cream, until charred and just cooked. Serve with steamed rice.

AFRICOLA STAFF MEAL MEAT SAUCE AND SPAGHETTI

SERVES 8

This is an excellent recipe to cook for the family. Even if you somehow avoid reproducing, I would recommend you cook the entire recipe for yourself and eat it while watching *Goodfellas* or *The Godfather* or the hanging footage of Benito Mussolini on YouTube.

INGREDIENTS

1 tbsp lard or beef dripping
50 g (2 oz) pancetta, diced
2 onions, diced
2 carrots, chopped
½ celery stalk, finely diced
3 tbsp finely diced garlic, sliced with a razor
    blade so it liquefies in the pan
2 bay leaves
Pinch of saffron
1 bunch of basil, leaves torn
2 tsp thyme leaves
1 tsp oregano leaves
1 tsp marjoram leaves
1 tsp ground cinnamon
1 tsp ground nutmeg
250 g (9 oz) minced beef
250 g (9 oz) minced pork
250 g (9 oz) minced veal
2 sweet Italian sausages (hot), removed from
    their casings
6 osso bucco (marrow scraped out and reserved)
4 tbsp tomato paste (concentrated purée)
1 glass of red wine (Shiraz)
2 x 400 g (14 oz) tins plum tomatoes
250 ml (1 cup) beef stock
100 ml (scant ½ cup) thick (double) cream
2 tbsp unsalted butter
3 tbsp flat-leaf parsley, chopped
1 packet of spaghetti
100 g (1 cup) freshly grated parmesan cheese
100 g (1 cup) freshly grated pecorino cheese
Sea salt and freshly ground black pepper

METHOD

In a large pot, heat the lard over medium–high heat. Add the pancetta and cook, stirring, for 4–5 minutes until browned and the fat is rendered.

Add the onion, carrot and celery and cook, stirring, for 4–5 minutes until soft. Add the garlic, 1 tablespoon sea salt, ½ teaspoon freshly ground black pepper, the bay leaves, saffron, basil, thyme, oregano, marjoram, cinnamon and nutmeg and cook, stirring, for just 30 seconds. Add the mince in batches and the sausage. Cook, stirring until no longer pink, for about 5 minutes or until slightly caramelised, then add the marrow.

Add 2 tablespoons of the tomato paste and cook, stirring, for 3–5 minutes. Pour in the wine and cook for about 2 minutes, stirring, to deglaze the pan, remove any browned bits sticking to the bottom of the pan and until half of the liquid is reduced.

Add the plum tomatoes with their juices, the remaining tomato paste and the beef stock and bring to the boil. Reduce the heat to medium–low and simmer for about 3 hours, stirring occasionally to prevent the sauce from sticking to the bottom of the pan, until thickened. If the sauce is looking a little dry, top up with more stock, otherwise your guests might make you sleep with the fishes if the sauce catches.

Add the cream, butter and parsley, stir well and simmer for 2 minutes. Adjust the seasoning to taste. Remove from the heat and cover to keep warm until ready to serve. Alternatively, hide in the kitchen, grab fresh bread and start working your way through the fat that settles on the top of the sauce. It's so delicious.

Meanwhile, bring salted water to the boil in a large pot. Add the pasta and return the water to a low boil. Cook, stirring occasionally to prevent the spaghetti from sticking, until al dente (8–10 minutes). Drain in a colander. I don't need to explain what happens next: serve the food with the grated cheese, eat.

* FEED ME * $75 PER PERSO

WINES

JUNGLE CURRY

SERVES 4

This recipe was inspired by my favourite Thai chef who isn't Thai, Ben Cooper from famed Melbourne restaurant Chin Chin. He probably sent me this recipe when we cooked together that one time, who knows? I didn't cut and paste this from an earlier email. I also didn't change the obvious protein of pork to panda so he wouldn't notice.

FROM: BENJAMIN COOPER
<BENJAMIN.COOPER@CHINCHIN.COM.AU>
SUBJECT: RECIPE
DATE: 10 APRIL 2018 AT 11:12:21 AM ACST
TO: HOLLY LUCAS <HOLLY.LUCAS@CHINCHIN.COM.AU>
CC: DUNCAN WELGEMOED <CHEF@AFRICOLA.COM>

HEY CHEF,
HERE'S THE RECIPE FOR OUR LUNCH TOGETHER,
ANY QUESTIONS GIVE ME A CALL.

50 g rendered pork fat
40 g pickled turmeric + garlic
250 g thinly sliced jungle meats, like panda or
   even pork fillet or something
100–150 g jungle curry paste
45 g shredded krachai
40 g crushed peanuts
10 g kaffir lime leaf, thinly sliced
60 g scud chilli – rough chopped
100 ml tamarind water
60 ml lime juice
10–20 g caster sugar
400 ml chicken stock
80 ml fish sauce
100 g baby corn – roll cut
50 g pea eggplant
60 g apple eggplant – thick sliced
50 g snake beans – cut into inch lengths
20 g holy basil
20 g Thai basil
50 g finely sliced bird's eye chillies
100 g toasted chopped peanuts
50 g crispy shallots

METHOD

Heat the rendered pork fat in a wide, heavy-based saucepan.

Then add the pickled turmeric and garlic and fry until fragrant. Add the panda.

Add the jungle paste, krachai, peanuts, lime leaf and chopped scud chilli.

Continue to fry until fragrant. Deglaze the pan with ½ the tamarind + lime juice and sugar. Add chicken stock and fish sauce and bring to the boil.

Add the vegetables and check the seasoning, and then add the remaining tamarind and lime juice as necessary.

Finish with the holy basil and Thai basil, chilli, peanuts and crisp shallots.

Looking forward to seeing you in Adelaide when we come and cook with you at Africola.

Make sure all the ordering is done before my arrival and the tequila is on ice.

Kind Regards

Benjamin Cooper

Executive chef
Chin Chin Melbourne, Sydney

CORNED BEEF AND HASH

SERVES 4

This recipe is dedicated to my mum. She loved cooking this up on a Sunday evening when we couldn't be arsed to cook something crazy after a large Sunday roast was consumed for lunch. I like my hash with crisp edges, heaps of ketchup and a couple of fried eggs on hot buttered toast.

This dish is the food equivalent of Rick Astley's 'Never Gonna Give You Up'.

INGREDIENTS

500 g (18 oz) tin corned beef
60 ml (¼ cup) Worcestershire sauce
1 tbsp ketchup
1 garlic clove, crushed
2 tbsp English mustard
1 kg (2 lb 4 oz) good mashing potatoes, peeled and halved
Vegetable oil, for frying
1 onion, thinly sliced and then slices halved
80 g (⅓ cup) unsalted butter
Sea salt and heaps of freshly ground white pepper

METHOD

Start by cutting the corned beef in half lengthways, then, using a sharp knife, cut into rough dice.

Put the corned beef in a bowl. Combine the Worcestershire sauce, ketchup, garlic and mustard in a cup and pour this all over the beef, mixing it around to distribute it evenly.

Pour enough boiling water from the kettle to almost cover the potatoes, then add salt and a lid and simmer for just 15 minutes before draining them in a colander.

Now heat 2 tablespoons of the oil in a frying pan and, when it's smoking hot, add the onion and toss it around in the oil to brown for about 3 minutes, keeping the heat high as they need to be very well browned at the edges. After that, push all the onion to the edge of the pan and, still keeping the heat very high, add the potato and flatten out with a spatula. Add a little more oil and the butter. Add salt and pepper and keep turning the potato and onion over as they start to catch.

After about 6 minutes, add the beef and continue to toss everything around to allow the beef to catch a little as well before serving.

BILTONG

★ ★ ★

MAKES 4

The snack of the gods and pretty much my favourite thing to eat ever. Not to be confused with jerky. Biltong is epic and jerky ... well ... jerky is a bit shit really. Biltong is also highly nutritious and a fantastic source of protein. It's basically paleo porn.

Biltong lasts approximately 9 seconds in my home as both my children and myself inhale it. Give it a whirl.

INGREDIENTS

1 kg (2 lb 4 oz) red meat (such as ostrich, venison, kangaroo, beef rump or flank)
60 ml (¼ cup) white vinegar
1 tbsp sea salt
55 g (¼ cup) brown sugar
40 g (1½ oz) coriander seeds, roughly crushed using a mortar and pestle
½ teaspoon freshly ground black pepper

EQUIPMENT

Large non-reactive tray
String
Electric fan

METHOD

Wash the meat, dry well on paper towel and cut at a slight angle to the grain into roughly 2.5 cm (1 inch) strips.

Sprinkle with 1 tablespoon of the vinegar and toss to coat.

Combine the salt, brown sugar, coriander and pepper in a large bowl, add the meat and toss well to coat. Transfer to a large, non-reactive tray and refrigerate for 8 hours, or overnight. Drain any excess blood after a few hours.

Combine the remaining vinegar with about 2 tablespoons water in a large bowl. Dip the biltong quickly into the vinegar mixture to remove some of the spiced salt. Make a very small incision into one end of each meat strip. Cut the string into 20 cm (8 inch) pieces, and thread a piece through each hole, tying to form a loop.

Hang the biltong over a rod or on hooks, close to an exposed light (to warm the air and lower humidity), with an electric fan circulating and blowing constantly on low speed over the meat. Leave to dry for 4–7 days, depending on the biltong size, humidity, temperature and preferred dryness. Cover and refrigerate once dried.

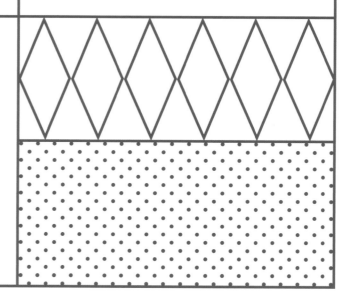

KANGAROO AND PULSES

SERVES 4

Kangaroo should be eaten by everyone. This recipe is an easy introduction to the animal. Only buy fresh and of the highest quality ... no roadkill.

INGREDIENTS

2 kangaroo loins
100 ml (scant ½ cup) red wine
2 garlic cloves, crushed
1 bird's eye chilli, chopped
1 sprig of rosemary, and 4 sprigs for the barbecue
1 tbsp soy sauce
25 g (1 oz) dried white peas (safed matar), soaked overnight
25 g (1 oz) adzuki beans, soaked overnight
25 g (1 oz) puy lentils
25 g (1 oz) cracked wheat
25 g (1 oz) quinoa (red and white)
2 carrots, finely diced
2 leeks, finely diced
2 celery stalks, finely diced
Oil, for frying
1 sprig of thyme, leaves picked
2 tsp sherry vinegar
200 ml (generous ¾ cup) brown chicken stock (preferably freshly made but bought is A-OK)
1 bunch of dill, leaves picked
1 bunch of marjoram, leaves picked
1 bunch of chives, finely chopped
Sea salt and freshly ground black pepper

EQUIPMENT

Barbecue

METHOD

Lay the kangaroo in a deep tray and add the red wine, garlic, chilli, sprig of rosemary and the soy sauce. Let the meat marinate for a few hours. Light the barbecue.

Individually cook the peas, beans and lentils in boiling water, as each will differ in timing. The white peas should take 1½ hours, the adzuki beans 1 hour and the puy lentils 45 minutes. The cracked wheat and the quinoa need 10–15 minutes.

Sweat the carrot, leek and celery in a little oil. Add the thyme and sherry vinegar, then the peas, beans, lentils and grains along with the stock. Bring to the boil and simmer until half the stock has evaporated. Season and finish with the herbs. It should be rich and clean tasting.

Once the coals have ashed over, lay the rosemary sprigs over the grill and the kangaroo on top of that. Not only will the rosemary protect the roo from flare ups, it will gently smoke the loin as it cooks. Grill for only a couple of minutes each side, making sure you get some even colour on the roo.

I like to serve the roo on the rarer side of medium-rare and rest it for 12–15 minutes.

Carve the roo and serve with the grains.

PIE SANGA BY WINEMAKER JOE HOLLYMAN

Vintage time in the winery is very busy, and sometimes you just have to eat what is easy to make. In 2015 we had a friend from Sydney come and help for a while and he introduced me to The Pie Sandwich.

It was a revelation, but over time I have played with the ingredients and my chef friends tell me if you change the recipe by 10 per cent, then you can call it your own.

Wine suggestion: cheap, cold, flavourless beer.

For an Asian fusion sandwich, you can swap the mayo for Kewpie mayo and the ketchup for Sriracha, which makes it a bit like an Aussie banh mi.

INGREDIENTS

Pies – my preference is beef, cheese and bacon
Cheap, sweet, fresh white bread – if it's a day old, it is too old!
Whole-egg mayonnaise
Tomato ketchup
Butter

METHOD

I prefer to warm the pies in the microwave and then finish them off in the oven – it means they do not get too dry or crunchy.

Generously cover one piece of bread with mayonnaise and then top with ketchup. Place pie on bread, add some more ketchup to taste, then cover with the other piece of bread, which you have generously spread with butter.

DURBAN LAMB NECK CURRY

SERVES 4

A Durban curry should be hot and sweet, like my Instagram selfies. This is seriously one of the most underrated curries in the curry encyclopaedia and should be eaten a day or two after it has actually been cooked. It gets better with age, unlike using social media references in a recipe introduction for a cookbook.

INGREDIENTS

5 tbsp ghee
1 kg (2 lb 4 oz) neck of lamb, diced
2 onions, finely diced
4 garlic cloves, finely diced
5 cm (2 inch) piece of fresh ginger,
   peeled and finely diced
6 tsp garam masala
3 tbsp Kashmiri chilli powder
250 g (9 oz) tinned chopped tomatoes
600 ml (2⅓ cups) lamb or chicken stock,
   mixed with 2 tbsp tomato paste
   (concentrated purée)
4 potatoes, quartered
3 green capsicums (peppers), trimmed and diced
20 dried apricots, soaked in hot water
   with 4 tbsp brown sugar
10 tbsp peas
Sea salt and freshly ground black pepper

METHOD

Heat the ghee in a cast-iron pan that has a lid and then add the diced lamb. Sauté the lamb in batches over medium heat until it is all browned, then set aside. Do not burn.

Add the onion, garlic and ginger to the pan and sauté over low heat until the onion is translucent. Turn the heat down to medium. Add the curry spices and cook for 1–2 minutes until they release their aroma.

Add the tinned tomatoes and stock with tomato paste and season to taste with salt. Simmer for 5 minutes before adding the potatoes. Cook until the potatoes are al dente (Italian for dented like a Fiat Uno driving along the Champs-Élysées), and then add the capsicum and apricots. Place a lid on the pan and simmer over low–medium heat, without boiling, for 35–40 minutes until the lamb is tender. Add the peas and season to taste.

ROASTED VENISON LOIN WITH MAPLE CARROTS AND CRISP SAGE

SERVES 2

This dish was cooked for Prince William and the Duchess of Cambridge on one of their very first dates when I was the chef of a gastropub called The Pot Kiln. They loved it; the many bookings we had to reschedule that evening weren't as chuffed. If you are finding it difficult to source venison, substitute the deer for kangaroo loin. Bonza mate.

INGREDIENTS

2 tbsp olive oil
250 g (9 oz) venison loin
2 tbsp unsalted butter
Sea salt and freshly ground black pepper

MADEIRA SAUCE

2 tbsp olive oil
6 French shallots, finely chopped
½ garlic bulb, cloves peeled and chopped
2 sprigs of thyme
1 bay leaf
10 button mushrooms, sliced
750 ml (3 cups) Madeira
6 dates, chopped
1.5 litres (6 cups) brown chicken stock
    (preferably freshly made but bought is A-OK)
2 tomatoes, halved
2 sprigs of tarragon

MAPLE CARROTS

2 carrots, peeled and quartered
4 baby carrots, left whole
2 tbsp olive oil
1 tbsp maple syrup

CRISP SAGE LEAVES

250 ml (1 cup) canola (rapeseed) oil
80 g (3 oz) sage leaves

METHOD

To prepare the Madeira sauce, heat the olive oil in a large saucepan over medium heat. Once the oil is hot, add the shallots, garlic, thyme and bay leaf to the pan and sauté for approximately 2 minutes, or until the shallots are soft. Add the mushrooms to the pan along with the Madeira and 2 of the chopped dates. Bring to the boil and reduce by two-thirds. Add the chicken stock and reduce by half. Add the tomatoes and tarragon to the pan, bring back to the boil and simmer for 15 minutes. Remove from the heat and skim the fat and impurities off the surface with a ladle. Pass the sauce through a sieve into a suitable container. Once cooled, store in the fridge.

Preheat the oven to 170°C (325°F). Place a roasting tray in the oven to warm.

Cook the carrots in boiling salted water for about 15 minutes. Place the carrots in the hot roasting tray and add the olive oil. Roast the carrots in the oven for 6–8 minutes, or until golden brown, turning them every 2 minutes. Add the maple syrup and place back in the oven for a further 2 minutes. Keep warm until required.

To make the crisp sage leaves, heat the canola oil to 180°C (350°F) in a medium saucepan, add the sage leaves and fry until crisp. Drain the leaves on paper towel.

To cook the venison, heat a frying pan until very hot and add the olive oil. Season the venison loin with salt and pepper and place straight into the pan. Seal the venison on all sides until golden brown. Add the butter to the pan and once it starts to foam, turn down the heat and cook for a further 2 minutes, continuously rolling the loin in the butter. For well-cooked venison, allow another 4–5 minutes. Remove from the pan and leave to rest. Season to taste with salt and pepper.

Gently reheat the Madeira sauce. Carve the venison and lay on the plate, followed by the remaining chopped dates, maple carrots, sage leaves and a good drizzle of sauce. Serve immediately.

POSH CHOPPED LIVER PÂTÉ

SERVES 12

This dish was the first thing I ate that truly made me want to be a chef – the livers were replaced with foie gras, mind you. It was so glorious that it made me weep pure Burgundy. Slum it with chicken livers though, it's almost as good. Peasants.

INGREDIENTS

Oil, for greasing
1 kg (2 lb 4 oz) chicken livers, cleaned
13 eggs, left out to room temperature
1 kg (2 lb 4 oz) unsalted butter, melted
   and kept warm
Sea salt and freshly ground white pepper

TERRINE REDUCTION

100 ml (scant ½ cup) Madeira
100 ml (scant ½ cup) tawny port
100 ml (scant ½ cup) dry sherry
3 French shallots, finely chopped
2 peppercorns
2 juniper berries
1 bay leaf

METHOD

Put all the ingredients for the reduction into a saucepan and reduce by half, then pass through a sieve and keep warm.

Take a deep baking dish, pour a little oil into it and grease the sides. On the kitchen bench, lay down one large layer of plastic wrap, saran wrap, cling film or whatever you call it in your country of origin. Put another layer of plastic wrap over the first sheet and smooth over so no air bubbles are trapped in it.

Place into the greased dish, making sure it's flush with the dish. There should be some overhang as this will be draped over to protect the top of the pâté from the heat of the oven.

Preheat the oven to 150°C (300°F).

To make the pâté, place the chicken livers in a blender and blitz until smooth. Add the eggs and 150 ml (generous ½ cup) of the terrine reduction and blend until incorporated. At this point you have to work pretty quick as the temperature of this meat slush will start to cool and if left too long before adding your butter, the mixture will split.

Keeping the blender on medium spin, slowly add the butter in a steady stream as if you were making a meat mayonnaise. The mixture should be smooth and at this point, add the salt and freshly ground white pepper. When I do this, I taste the mixture raw, which might be gross to some people. You don't have to do this. I'll think less of you if you don't, though.

Once seasoned, pass through a sieve to trap any veins or sinew or egg gunge. Pour the mixture into your dish and pull the plastic wrap tight to trap any potential air bubbles that might form.

Fold the plastic wrap over the mixture, place the dish into a deep baking tray and fill with hot water so it reaches the sides of the dish, trying to fill it to the pâté level. Hot tip: do this when the dish is in the oven.

Bake for 1 hour-ish, checking every 30 minutes to see how you go. What you are looking for is a firm wobble, like a crème brûlée. Once cooked, chill in the fridge overnight.

Spoon big lumps of the pâté onto toasted challah and serve with your favourite fruit compote, or caviar and truffle, if you're a baller.

CRYING TIGER

SERVES 2

Australia is hotter than the sun on a good day, so this recipe is perfect for those sweltering afternoons. Spicy, fragrant, bitter and sour ... just how I like my friends.

BO TAI CHANH

225 g (8 oz) fillet steak
¼ lemon
1 lime, cut into wedges
½ tsp sea salt, plus more as needed
¼ tsp cracked Kampot pepper or coarsely
    ground black pepper, plus more as needed
1 handful of rau ram (Vietnamese coriander)
20 g (1 cup) mint leaves
30 g (1 cup) coriander (cilantro) leaves
30 g (1 cup) Thai basil leaves
¼ red onion, thinly sliced
1 red Asian shallot, thinly sliced
¼ serrano chilli, thinly sliced
2 tbsp store-bought or homemade fried shallots

NUOC CHAM

60 ml (¼ cup) fish sauce
60 g (¼ cup) sugar
2 tbsp rice vinegar
1 tbsp lime juice
1 tbsp lemon juice
1 tsp peeled and grated fresh ginger
1 tsp minced red Asian shallot
1 tsp minced garlic
1 tsp minced lemongrass

METHOD

About 30 minutes before serving, place the beef in the freezer; you want it to be partially frozen so that it's easy to slice thinly.

In a bowl or jar, stir all the ingredients for the nuoc cham together until the sugar is dissolved. Refrigerate until ready to use.

Remove the beef from the freezer and slice the meat against the grain into 12 very thin slices. Use the side of your knife or a meat mallet to flatten any thick or uneven slices.

Place the beef on a baking sheet. Squeeze the lemon and half of the lime wedges over the top and drizzle with half the nuoc cham. Sprinkle with the salt and pepper. Let sit for 5–10 minutes.

Meanwhile, combine the rau ram, mint, coriander, Thai basil, red onion, shallot and chilli in a large bowl. Dress with 1 tablespoon of the nuoc cham, and toss to combine.

Add the beef slices one at a time to the bowl, being careful to avoid clumping. Add a little more nuoc cham and toss to coat. Sprinkle 1 tablespoon of the fried shallots over the top of the salad and toss again to combine.

Pile the salad onto a serving plate. Drizzle with more nuoc cham, sprinkle with more salt and pepper if needed, and top with the remaining fried shallots. Serve with the remaining lime wedges.

PEANUT BUTTER BURGERS

SERVES 8 KIDS

I had to include a recipe for the two things my kids love: burgers and peanut butter. I know this seems slightly odd, but not if you're a child – just think of the peanut butter as a less sophisticated satay sauce. This recipe isn't for anyone with a peanut allergy; in fact if you do have one, turn the fucking page. Quickly.

INGREDIENTS

Drop or two of peanut (groundnut) oil
1 kg (2 lb 4 oz) freshly ground chuck steak
240 g (1 cup) creamy peanut butter
Dill pickles
8 soft white buns, toasted
Sea salt and freshly ground black pepper

METHOD

Heat a cast-iron skillet over medium heat and add a drop or two of peanut oil. Use the spatula to spread the oil, coating the cooking surface.

Place the ground beef in a mixing bowl with heaps of black pepper and form eight balls of beef, placing them on the heated skillet as you go. Each ball should have about 7 cm (2¾ inches) of space around it. You may only be able to cook two or three burgers at a time.

Add a generous pinch of salt to each ball of beef and then, using a stiff spatula, press them down hard until they become wide patties just a bit larger than the buns. Let them cook, undisturbed, for 2½ minutes or until reddish liquid begins to form on the surface of the patties.

As soon as the patties are smashed, heat the peanut butter in a small saucepan over low heat.

When the burgers are ready on the first side, flip each patty once and don't press them again. Spoon some of the warm peanut butter over the patties and cook for another 2 minutes or so.

Meanwhile, add a couple of sliced pickles to each bottom bun and set aside.

When the patties are cooked though, remove them from the heat and place them on the toasted buns.

To totally freak your kids out, finish with some strawberry jam.

DEEP-FRIED BOLOGNA

MAKES 2 BOLOGNA

This was the most popular dish at Africola when we opened for brunch in the early days of the restaurant. It has become a hospo cult dish of sorts. The recipe makes a lot, so freeze any leftover sausage for school lunches or pizza toppings.

INGREDIENTS

250 g (9 oz) pork fatback (back fat)
   (150 g/5½ oz cut into large cubes, and the
   rest cut into 5–6 mm (¼ inch) dice – get your
   butcher to do this)
2 small egg whites, briefly beaten
50 g (⅓ cup) pistachio nuts
1.75 kg (3 lb 14 oz) pork shoulder, finely minced
2 tsp pink salt (aka curing salt)
40 g (⅓ cup) sea salt flakes
1 tbsp paprika
½ tsp ground nutmeg
½ tsp almond extract
125 g (generous 1 cup) dried milk powder
125 g (4½ oz) frozen full-cream milk
  (buy fresh milk and freeze)
60 ml (¼ cup) amaretto
60 ml (¼ cup) port
1 tbsp ground Kampot peppercorns
Oil, for frying
Sea salt

CRUMBS

100 g (3½ cups) plain flour
2 eggs, whisked
250 g (9 oz) Japanese breadcrumbs

EQUIPMENT

Cooking thermometer

METHOD

Blanch the small-diced fatback in simmering water for 5 minutes, then chill in ice water. Drain and toss the fat in a bowl with the egg whites and pistachios.

Combine the larger chunks of fatback with the pork in a chilled bowl. Sprinkle on the pink and sea salt, paprika, nutmeg, almond extract and milk powder. Divide your mince into two bowls. Crush the frozen milk in a plastic bag and add it to the meat with the amaretto and port. Purée until it's as smooth as your machine will make it. Test a lump of meat by poaching for a couple of minutes in a pan of boiling water, then chilling it in an ice bath. Keep seasoning and testing by poaching until you have it just right.

Fold the peppercorns and the egg-white mixture into the two batches of purée. Let them cure, covered, in the fridge for 2 days.

Lay each portion of meat in the centre of a wide piece of plastic wrap, pull the wrap around it, roll into a sausage-shaped cylinder and twist the ends as tightly as you can without bursting the package open. This is called a torchon in French.

Bring a large pot of water to a simmer and submerge the sausages. Cook for 1 hour or until a thermometer inserted into the centre says 75°C (167°F). Plunge the cooked sausages into an ice bath and chill completely. Dry and refrigerate overnight.

Slice into 4 cm (1½ inch) thick discs. Place the discs first into the flour, then the eggs and finally the breadcrumbs. Once crumbed, place the sausage discs into hot oil and deep-fry for 3–4 minutes until golden. Drain on paper towel and season with sea salt.

ALMOST BELLES FRIED CHICKEN

★ ★ ★

SERVES 2

There is only one king of fried chicken in Australia and that's our old friend Morgan McGlone. I've been eating this man's chicken for nearly a decade and it still blows me away. You will always find Morgs either in the kitchen at Belles or drinking a glass of natural wine at the bar, being the perfect host.

This recipe is our way more complicated version of his insane chicken. Salute brother.

INGREDIENTS

2 tbsp paprika
2 tbsp freshly ground black pepper
2 tsp garlic powder
2 tsp dried oregano
½ tsp cayenne pepper
2 skinless chicken breasts
250 ml (1 cup) buttermilk
1 tsp Peri peri sauce (page 20), plus
    extra to serve
1 large egg
1 tbsp table salt, plus 2 tsp for the flour
350 g (2⅓ cups) plain flour
120 g (1 cup) cornflour
1 tsp baking powder
1 litre (4 cups) vegetable shortening or
    peanut (groundnut) oil
White bread, pickles, maple syrup and caviar,
    to serve

EQUIPMENT

Large gallon-sized zip-lock bags
Deep fryer or large pot
Cooking thermometer

METHOD

Place the paprika, pepper, garlic, oregano and cayenne in a bowl and mix well with a fork.

Sandwich each piece of chicken between two pieces of plastic wrap or inside an opened zip-lock bag and pound with a meat pounder or heavy skillet until 5 mm (¼ inch) thick.

Whisk the buttermilk, peri peri, egg, salt and 2 tablespoons of the spice mixture in a bowl. Add the chicken and turn to coat. Transfer the contents to a large zip-lock bag and refrigerate for at least 4 hours or overnight, flipping the bag occasionally to redistribute the contents and coat the chicken evenly.

Whisk together the flour, cornflour, baking powder, remaining salt and spice mixture in a bowl. Add 3 tablespoons of marinade from the zip-lock bag and work into the flour with your fingertips. Remove the chicken from the bag, allowing excess buttermilk to drip off. Drop the chicken into the flour mix and toss until thoroughly coated, pressing with your hand to get the flour to adhere in a thick layer. Shake the chicken over the bowl to remove excess flour, then transfer to a plate.

Adjust an oven rack to the middle position in the oven and preheat to 150°C (300°F).

Heat the shortening in a large pot or deep fryer for 6 minutes or until a medium–high heat of 220°C (450°F) has been reached. Maintain the temperature, being careful not to let the fat get any hotter. Lower two pieces of chicken into the pot. Now adjust the heat to 162°C (324°F). Fry the chicken without moving for 2 minutes, then carefully agitate with a wire-mesh spider or tongs, making sure not to knock off any breading, and cook for 3 minutes until the bottom is deep golden brown. Carefully flip and continue to cook for 2 minutes until the second side is golden.

Transfer the chicken to a paper towel-lined plate to drain for 30 seconds, flipping once, then transfer to a wire rack set over a baking tray. Serve with white bread, pickles, peri peri sauce, maple syrup and caviar and then think about your life choices ... you dirty bugger.

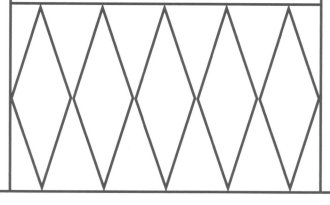

SIRLOIN STEAK SALAD WITH CHICORY AND ANCHOVIES

SERVES 4

This is a perfect summer salad in my opinion. Grab yourself some dry-aged sirloin and give this recipe a whirl.

ANCHOVY DRESSING

1 small egg yolk
2 tsp Dijon mustard
1 generous tbsp red wine vinegar
30 g (1 oz) good-quality tinned anchovies in oil, drained (reserve the oil)
½ garlic clove, finely chopped
Sriracha, to taste
150 ml (generous ½ cup) sunflower oil
2 tsp lemon juice
Sea salt flakes and freshly ground black pepper

SIRLOIN AND CHICORY

1 head of red chicory
1 French shallot, thinly sliced
250 g (9 oz) sirloin steak, sliced
Extra virgin olive oil
1 tbsp red wine vinegar
90 g (¾ cup) walnuts, chopped and toasted

METHOD

For the anchovy dressing, place the egg yolk, mustard, vinegar, anchovies and garlic in a bowl or food processor. Add a few dashes of Sriracha and a good pinch of salt and pepper. Blend to combine.

With the motor still running, slowly drizzle in the anchovy oil, then the sunflower oil and finally 2 teaspoons of water and the lemon juice.

Cut the chicory lengthways and, using the tip of your knife, remove the core. Slice it at an angle into bite-sized pieces. Place in a mixing bowl with the shallot.

Cover the steak in olive oil and season. Cook the steak on a hot chargrill pan for about 1 minute each side (depending on how you like your steak cooked). Add the red wine vinegar to the pan. Let it sizzle for a few seconds, then remove the meat and set aside.

Dress the chicory salad with 6 tablespoons of the dressing and toss it well, then top with the walnuts and serve alongside your sweet-and-sour and umami AF steak.

TANDOORI BUTLER STEAK

SERVES 2

Butler steak – also known as flat iron or oyster blade – is one of the tastiest cuts of beef. I've put two methods of cookery, one that's just an everyday method and one that's actually super weird, but way better flavour wise.

INGREDIENTS

2 tbsp mustard seeds
2 tbsp fennel seeds
2 tbsp freshly ground black pepper
1 tbsp Kampot peppercorns
1½ tbsp sea salt flakes
1 tsp hot pepper flakes
¼ tsp cayenne pepper
2 large butler steaks, fascia (membrane) removed
1 tbsp extra virgin olive oil

EQUIPMENT

Barbecue (optional)
Firelighters
Dried logs, like iron bark or red gum

METHOD

Add the mustard seeds, fennel seeds and the black and Kampot pepper to a dry frying pan and cook for 1–3 minutes until fragrant and lightly toasted, stirring with a wooden spoon. Do not let burn. Transfer the spices to a heatproof bowl to cool, then place in a spice grinder. Grind in short bursts until a coarse powder forms. Add the salt, pepper flakes and cayenne.

Brush the meat on all sides with the olive oil and generously season with the spice rub.

If using a barbecue, place firelighters under a few pieces of dried log in the barbecue and burn until the whole logs are red hot and glowing. Place the logs on top of the grill and place the meat straight on top of the wood. This acts like a ghetto tandoor and works perfectly because the flavour of the wood permeates through the beef. Brown for 3–4 minutes each side, then rest.

If using a grill, heat to high and cook the meat until evenly caramelised on both sides – about 5 minutes total for medium–rare.

KANGAROO POTJIE

SERVES 4

Kangaroo is one of the biggest protein resources in the world and Australians just don't eat enough of it. Kangaroo meat is sublime and I've included a method I learnt in the outback for defurring the tails. This is a weird South African, Australian fusion – sums me up really.

INGREDIENTS

4 kangaroo tails
Olive oil, for searing
2 whole cloves
1 cinnamon stick
1 tsp coriander seeds
4 cardamom pods, crushed
1 tsp chilli flakes
5 fresh curry leaves
1 tsp good madras curry powder
1 tbsp biryani spice or madras curry powder
5 fresh bay leaves
2 large onions, sliced
2 garlic cloves, chopped
1 piece of fresh ginger, peeled and chopped
1 chilli, seeded and chopped
2 leeks, diced
2 carrots, diced
1 sweet potato, diced
1 celeriac, diced
150 ml (generous ½ cup) red wine (Shiraz)
150 ml (generous ½ cup) chicken stock
1 small piece of lemon zest
Sea salt and freshly ground black pepper
Knobs of butter, to finish
1 bunch of flat-leaf parsley, finely chopped, to finish
Crusty bread, to serve

EQUIPMENT

Charcoal barbecue

METHOD

Throw the kangaroo tails into the coals while there is still a flame and singe off all the hair. It should take about 15 minutes for all of the fur to burn off. Skin and then saw into portions. The portions will be dictated by each joint in the tail – just cut straight through between the joints.

Seal the meat in olive oil in a large cast-iron pot over the fire until it's browned, then remove from the pot. Add the spices and toast until you can smell them. Add the onion, garlic, ginger, chilli and all the vegetables and sweat. Return the meat to the pot.

Deglaze with the red wine, reduce by half, then add the stock and lemon zest.

Cook over embers for 3 hours or until the roo is tender. Season and finish with the butter and parsley. Serve with crusty bread.

RIB OF BEEF AND N'DOLE

SERVES 4

This is one of those big dick banger recipes.
I normally have this with a MASSIVE, GROSS RED
WINE FROM THE BAROSSA VALLEY BECAUSE
I'M A HEATHEN AND DON'T CARE. Enjoy.

INGREDIENTS

1 kg (2 lb 4 oz) rib-eye rack of aged beef
3 onions, finely chopped
2 garlic cloves, finely chopped
2 bird's eye chillies, finely chopped
1 tbsp biryani spice or a good
    madras curry powder
200 g (7 oz) kapenta or ikan bilis (dried Lake
    Tanganyika sardines, available from selected
    African food stores, or substitute with ikan bilis,
    available from Asian food stores)
500 g (1 lb 2 oz) golden chard or any Swiss chard
1 kg (2 lb 4 oz) spinach, roughly chopped
Olive oil, for brushing
Sea salt and freshly ground black pepper
Flat breads and pickled vegetables, to serve

HAM HOCK

1 hock bone
1 bunch of thyme
2 whole cloves
1 carrot, roughly chopped
1 onion, roughly chopped
1 bunch of celery leaves

EQUIPMENT

Charcoal barbecue

METHOD

Put all the ingredients for the ham hock in a pot
with 1 litre (4 cups) water and bring to the boil for
2 hours. Pass through a fine mesh sieve and reserve
250 ml (1 cup) for the cooking.

Take the rib out of the fridge and allow to come to
room temperature.

To make the n'dole, sweat the onion, garlic, chilli
and the biryani spice in a deep pot. Add the
kapenta/ikan bilis and cook for a further 5 minutes.

Add the chard and spinach and cook until all the
water has evaporated. Deglaze the pot with the ham
hock stock and season to taste.

Light the fire on the barbecue and wait until the
coals have ashed. Brush the rib of beef with olive
oil and caramelise one side, then flip over and
caramelise the other side. Continue flipping from
side to side for 15 minutes, brushing with olive oil.
Leave to rest for 7½ minutes. Season liberally with
salt and pepper.

Carve the beef and serve with n'dole. Flat breads
and pickled vegetables work well as a side too.

OXTAIL POTJIE

SERVES 4

The Voortrekkers altered the Dutch oven to make it round and with a large metal handle for hanging on the back of a wagon. The pioneers shot wild game, of which there was fucking heaps as you can imagine being in Africa, and the potjie provided a good way of using up the meat scraps and bones. Each day when the wagons stopped, the pot was placed over a fire to simmer. New bones replaced old and fresh meat replaced meat eaten. It was like an African master stock of sorts. The pot was never washed, but always on the boil whenever the wagons stopped.

The pot can be heated using small amounts of twisted grass or even dried animal dung like in the olden days, so when the apocalypse eventually comes, which to be fair could be any day now, keep this useful fact in the back of your head if you're one of the lucky few not to be eaten by the zombies.

Also, if the world has ended and you're one of those survival Mormons reading this, this recipe is perfectly suited for large families.

INGREDIENTS

1 tsp good madras curry powder
1 tsp sea salt
1 tsp smoked paprika
1 tsp coriander seeds, crushed
1 tsp freshly ground black pepper
1 kg (2 lb 4 oz) oxtail pieces, as lean as possible
60 ml (¼ cup) olive oil
2 onions, finely chopped
6 garlic cloves, crushed
250 ml (1 cup) stout
1 tbsp honey
1 tsp ground cinnamon
1 tsp ground allspice
1 litre (4 cups) beef or chicken stock
3 carrots, peeled and cut into large dice
1 small butternut squash, peeled and cut into
  large dice
400 g (14 oz) tin plum tomatoes
1 bunch of thyme
Mrs Balls Chutney, to finish
Sea salt and freshly ground black pepper

METHOD

Put the curry powder, salt, paprika, coriander and pepper into a plastic bag and toss together with the oxtail pieces so the meat is evenly coated.

Heat the olive oil in a large, flat-bottomed potjie or heavy-bottomed cast-iron pot. Add the onion and garlic and fry for a few minutes until just turning brown. Add the oxtail and brown all over.

Once the meat is sealed, add the stout, honey, the rest of the spices, half the stock, the carrot, squash, tomatoes and thyme. Cover the pot and cook slowly over a very low heat for 3 hours.

Every so often, check to see that there's enough liquid and add stock if needed to prevent it drying out. The meat and vegetables should be covered. Keep checking to ensure there's enough moisture until the meat is soft and the vegetables have disintegrated.

Season to taste with sea salt and black pepper and add a little chutney into the potjie for sweetness.

GREEN CHICKEN CURRY

SERVES 4

I included this recipe because I think it's very important to understand Thai methods of cookery and how you can apply their particular techniques to your everyday repertoire. I know some of these ingredients might not seem familiar, but take the plunge and experiment. Let your taste buds do the talking on this one.

INGREDIENTS

500 ml (2 cups) coconut cream
2½ tbsp coconut oil
1½ tbsp finely shaved light palm sugar (jaggery), or to taste
80 ml (⅓ cup) fish sauce, or to taste
10 skinless chicken thigh fillets, cut into bite-sized pieces
3 litres (12 cups) coconut milk
250 ml (1 cup) chicken stock
400 g (14 oz) apple eggplants (aubergines), halved, or pea eggplants (aubergines)
25 g (½ cup) Thai basil
8 makrut (kaffir lime) leaves, coarsely torn, plus extra whole leaves to serve
3 long red chillies, thickly sliced diagonally, plus extra to serve
2 tbsp fried shallots (homemade or bought)
2 tbsp fried garlic (homemade or bought)
Jasmine rice and lime wedges, to serve

GREEN CURRY PASTE

15 coriander (cilantro) roots
10 green bird's eye chillies, finely chopped
¼ tsp sea salt
3 lemongrass stems, white part only, thinly sliced
2 cm (¾ inch) piece of fresh galangal, peeled and finely chopped
2 tsp fresh turmeric, finely chopped
Zest of 1½ makruts (kaffir limes), pith discarded, green part finely chopped
4 red Asian shallots, finely chopped
4 garlic cloves, finely chopped
1 tsp shrimp paste, roasted (wrap in foil and roast in the oven on high for 5–10 minutes)
10 white peppercorns
½ tsp coriander seeds, dry-roasted and ground
1 tsp cumin seeds, dry-roasted and ground

EQUIPMENT

Mortar and pestle or Thermomix

METHOD

First, make the curry paste. Scrape the fibrous outer layer from the coriander roots, soak in a bowl of cold water for 5 minutes to remove grit, then drain, rinse, finely chop and set aside.

Pound the bird's eye chilli and salt to a fine paste using a mortar and pestle for 5 minutes.

One at a time, add the coriander root, lemongrass, galangal, turmeric, makrut (kaffir lime) zest, shallot and garlic, pounding each to a fine paste before adding the next ingredient. Add the shrimp paste, pound to combine, then add the peppercorns and pound until finely crushed. Add the ground coriander and cumin seeds, pound to combine and set aside. Alternatively, just chuck it all in a Thermomix and hope for the best.

Simmer the coconut cream and coconut oil in a large saucepan over low–medium heat, stirring frequently, for about 5–10 minutes until thickened and the oil rises to the surface. Don't freak out, it's supposed to look split.

Add half the curry paste (freeze what you don't use) and stir for 4–5 minutes until fragrant and deepened in colour. Add the sugar and cook for 2–3 minutes until lightly caramelised, then add the fish sauce and stir to combine.

Add the chicken and stir for 2–3 minutes to coat well. Add the coconut milk and stock, stir to combine, then add the eggplants and simmer for 4–5 minutes until the chicken is cooked and the eggplants are just tender. Add the Thai basil, makrut (kaffir lime) leaves and chilli, adjust the seasoning to taste and stir to combine.

Scatter with the fried shallots, fried garlic, the extra lime leaves and extra chilli and serve hot with steamed jasmine rice and lime wedges.

WHOLE SMOKED PIG

★ ★ ★

SERVES 12

The first time I cooked a pig this way I was cooking with pitmaster Rodney Scott for a local barbecue festival. I was put in charge of the pigs so it meant I was cooking for about 48 hours straight, which made me so tired I could literally see through time. There's not a better pig cook than Rodney in the world, in my opinion, and I was lucky enough to learn some of his secrets. The number one secret to his world-famous barbecue – get someone else to do it.

INGREDIENTS

8–10 kg (17–22 lb) suckling pig, butterflied
500 ml (2 cups) white distilled vinegar
80 g (3 oz) MSG
100 g (3½ oz) cracked white peppercorns
Sea salt

BRINE

460 g (1 lb) sea salt flakes
4 litres (16 cups) water
95 g (½ cup) brown sugar
225 ml (scant 1 cup) apple cider vinegar
2 bunches of thyme
10 fresh bay leaves
6 lemons, halved
4 garlic bulbs, halved

EQUIPMENT

Blowtorch
Large container or butcher's tub
2 barbecues (1 for cooking, 1 for making
    the fire – Webers work very well)
Pack of firelighters (we aren't f#kin' cavemen)
20 kg (45 lb) good compressed hardwood
    charcoal (I use Clean Heat barbecue coals
    from mopani tree wood, just to give you
    an idea; please avoid cheap charcoal)
10 kg (22 lb) dry wood, split
Large tray with a cooling rack
Shovel

METHOD

Grab a blowtorch and singe off any hairs around the pig's ears and belly. To make the brine, put all the ingredients in a large pot and bring to the boil, then take off the heat and cool. Place the pig in a large container or butcher's tub and pour over the brine. Brine for 24 hours, then pull out and dry very well.

Start your fire using firelighters and charcoal and, once the fire is raging hot, add wood and let it burn down to embers. This recipe will require constant top-ups of wood and coal so you have enough embers to cook your pig.

When you have a large amount of coal ashed and breaking into embers, shovel the embers into the second barbecue. Create a trench down the centre so the coals are only up the sides of the barbecue and not directly under the pig as this will create more of an even heat. Place the pig on the barbecue and close the lid, making sure all your vents are open to allow for constant airflow. Check every 30 minutes or so, topping up the embers and making sure it isn't burning. It takes about 3 hours to cook. Keep burning the coal and wood in the other barbecue. Once the belly and shoulders are soft to the point you can pull the meat off with a fork, take off the heat and place on a large tray with a rack to catch all those juices. Rest for 15 minutes.

Using your knife, take off the crackling in sheets. If the skin hasn't crackled, don't hate yourself, we can remedy this. Once the skin is taken off, use your shovel to disperse the embers so they are evenly spread. Place the skin on the grill rack, fatty-side up. It should take a few minutes to start crackling and bubbling. Pull off and put to one side.

Warm the vinegar, MSG, pepper and pork juices in a pan until the MSG is dissolved. Using a hand blender, emulsify until smooth. Pull off all the meat and roughly chop. Season with salt and drizzle over the vinegar emulsion, repeating until the meat is well seasoned and sharp as fuck. Chop the crackling, mix through the meat and serve.

Sustainability has become a buzz word and a marketing ploy. The term sustainability lost its weight the moment we started slapping it on products wrapped in plastic. It's lost its meaning and become another consumable for corporations to find loopholes in or to take advantage of. Is it even possible to sustain what we currently have? And more to the point, why the fuck would we want to sustain what we already have?

The oceans are heating up, ice caps are melting, wildlife is dying at an alarming rate, natural disasters are becoming an everyday occurrence and the Kardashians are still a fucking thing, while bees literally drop dead in waves. I'd also not be the first person to say, for measure, that pretending to destroy the economy in order to achieve a better system would be beneficial for everyone either, such as investing in renewable energy instead of coal. All I really know is that we can't sit still and emblazon the word 'sustainable' on every new product and hope that somehow these problems disappear.

Tackling these problems is over-whelmingly daunting. It's gotten to the point where the weight rests on all of the planet's woefully trout-shouldered homo sapiens to take charge as individuals. Can't win a Nobel Prize for popping out a Keynesian mastermind economic solution to environmentally and socially destructive economics? No worries! You can do small things. The first increment of any action has the greatest impact and any act that follows this has less and less. This is actually comforting. It means that all the small things you do in the beginning genuinely have a positive effect. We can collectively take a bunch of small, easy steps that become one massive incremental change. The only downer is that as you keep making changes, the impact is less shiny and marketable. That's not really a downer for the things that matter, but in terms of making it Instagrammable or sellable as a concept, it makes it much harder.

The reality is we all suck at being better people. It's hard to undo generations of consuming and wasting. Millennials, Gen X and Gen Y are all neurotic messes because we can literally smell death in the air, but feel like there are no tools to fix it. Even more confronting is that there is no global solution we can buy into. Everything has to be decentralised and dismantled. It has to start with things in your own backyard. Do the clichés: plant a garden, make bees happy, stop buying plastics, reduce your consumption, buy Birkenstocks, get on the Sea Shepherd and scream at the ocean like it's the nihilist void you've always dreamed of. And this overwhelming dread becomes a thousand times louder when you're a part of hospitality, trust me.

The biggest problem restaurants – and the world – face with these problems is the lack of transparency. Nobody REALLY wants to say the gross shit out loud about their restaurant. All we want to do is advertise the good and not have the discussion around it. Your seafood is local, but it's rocking up in Styrofoam. Your lettuce is organic, but it comes wrapped in plastic. You use local pottery, but it takes millions of litres of water a night to clean on the driest continent on Earth. Some stuff isn't our fault: some of it is health regulations and some of it is that we can't foot the cost of immediate change. The most uncomfortable part that you have to acknowledge about this industry, though, is that you're a main factor in excessive consumption. Even worse, it's excessive consumption wrapped up in glamour and TV shows and awards and, ahem, book deals, and there is a pressure to fit a pretty and uncomplicated version of sustainability. Nobody wants to hear a restaurant owner is going broke trying to use only organic produce. Nobody wants to hear that this week you had to cut corners and buy caged chicken. Customers don't want you to say to them, 'Sorry, tuna isn't available because it's an endangered species.' We can't address these problems because we can't openly discuss them as a community and help each other.

Africola has work to do on the environ-mental front. We compost, we recycle, we know as many of our farmers and wine makers as possible, we do as much as we can with the resources we have. But we could wind down our plastic use and be better on water consumption. We can do more and we want to. Every day is an opportunity to change. We genuinely believe that most people feel this way – especially our peers. Be brave, say the ugly thing: fuck sustainability.

02

LA MER

Fish

AT AFRICOLA, WE DON'T USE FANCY SEAFOOD. WE USE SEAFOOD
THAT IS PLENTIFUL, DIRECT FROM OUR FISHERMEN. WE TRY OUR
BEST NOT TO BUY BYCATCH BECAUSE THE INCIDENTAL CAPTURE
OF ANIMALS KILLS A STAGGERING AMOUNT OF MARINE LIFE – ALL
HAULED UP WITH THE TARGETED CATCH AND THEN DISCARDED
OVERBOARD – A COMPLETE WASTE OF LIFE THAT'S DETRIMENTAL TO
THE ENVIRONMENT. YOU ALSO WON'T FIND THE ENDANGERED TUNA
ANYWHERE NEAR MY MENU. WE CHAMPION THE HUMBLE MACKEREL
AND SARDINE. THE OILIER THE FISH, THE BETTER.

PIPIS, FERMENTED CHILLI BROTH

SERVES 4

This dish is a staple at the shop. We serve hundreds a week and it probably won't ever come off the menu until you lot cook it to death and eventually get bored of eating it.

INGREDIENTS

2 kg (4 lb 8 oz) Goolwa pipis or any small clams, cockles or even mussels

HOT BROTH

250 ml (1 cup) soy sauce
2½ tbsp kecap manis
1 scud or bird's eye chilli, chopped
2 garlic cloves, finely chopped
1 tsp peeled and grated fresh ginger
80 g (⅓ cup) unsalted butter
100 ml (scant ½ cup) dry cider
2 tbsp white wine vinegar
65 g (scant ½ cup) Israeli couscous, cooked
200 ml (generous ¾ cup) lemon juice
100 g (3½ oz) fennel tops, chopped
100 g (3½ oz) karkalla (or any other beach succulent such as samphire)
Sea salt flakes

METHOD

Soak your pipis in fresh water overnight.

Place the soy, kecap manis and chilli in a bowl and emulsify with a hand blender.

To make the broth, put a cast-iron pot over a fire or a heavy-based saucepan on the stove and fry the garlic and ginger in the butter until translucent.

Add the pipis and the cider and bring to the boil. Add the soy mixture and vinegar and season, add the cooked Israeli couscous, then chuck in heaps of lemon, the chopped fennel tops and the karkalla.

To serve, throw into a bowl and eat with crusty bread while using the shells as tiny spoons, you weirdo.

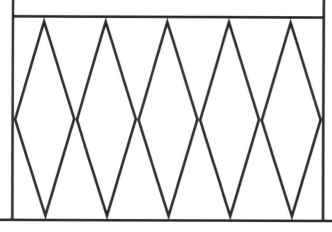

ROLLED AND MARINATED SARDINES

SERVES 4

Perfect as a quick snack or served alongside a salad for a delicious and easy starter.

INGREDIENTS

12 sardine fillets, cleaned

MARINADE

1 garlic bulb, cloves peeled and finely grated
20 kalamata olives
Zest of 2 lemons
500 ml (2 cups) olive oil, plus extra for brushing
Sea salt and freshly ground black pepper

METHOD

Blend all of the seasoning ingredients together in a food processor.

Brush the sardines on the flesh side with the seasoning and roll them up, skin-side out, from tail end to head end.

When you're ready to cook, skewer the sardines with a toothpick and brush with olive oil. Gently grill on a hot cast-iron skillet very quickly – just 2–3 minutes.

Serve straight away.

OYSTER CREAM AND POTATO CHIPS

SERVES 2

The ultimate chips and dips. Serve this to your friends at the next big game day.

INGREDIENTS

10 oysters, shucked and juices reserved
Juice of 2 lemons
250 ml (1 cup) rapeseed oil
Your favourite potato chips (preferably salt and vinegar)
A giant lump of caviar
Sea salt and freshly ground white pepper

EQUIPMENT

High-speed blender

METHOD

Put the oysters, their juices and the lemon juice into a high-speed blender and blend until smooth.

Slowly add the oil until the mixture starts to thicken, as you would making a mayonnaise.

Season with a little sea salt and heaps of white pepper.

Serve with chips and a giant lump of caviar.

HOT SMOKED MACKEREL AND HORSERADISH

SERVES 6

This method of smoking in your domestic kitchen can be used with a variety of fish or shellfish. Make sure you don't have ultra-sensitive smoke alarms. Also, have a tea towel handy as the smoke tray does get very hot.

INGREDIENTS

200 g (1½ cups) sea salt flakes
8 mackerel fillets
Coarsely ground or cracked black pepper
Olive oil, for greasing
A squeeze of lemon juice
Horseradish sauce

EQUIPMENT

A handful of smoking chips, such as hickory or
    maple wood, soaked in water overnight
Deep tray
Cooling rack
Foil

METHOD

Scatter half the salt onto a tray or plate. Place the mackerel on top. Scatter on the rest of the salt and leave for 5 minutes. Wash quickly and pat dry with paper towel. Season well with cracked black pepper.

Drain the smoking chips and place at the bottom of the deep tray, with the cooling rack on top.

Place the fish on the cooling rack, flesh-side down. I would recommend slightly greasing the underside of the fish with some olive oil to prevent sticking.

Cover the tray with the foil. Place the tray on two burners on medium heat. Once smoke starts to billow out of the foil, turn the heat down to low and smoke the mackerel for 5–10 minutes, until the flesh is opaque and flakes when pressed with a knife.

Lift off gently onto a plate and serve with a squeeze of lemon juice and a dollop of horseradish.

GUMMY SHARK BRANDADE, SOURDOUGH TOAST AND FRIED SALTBUSH

SERVES 4

This dish was created by famous Australian chef Mark Best and it was the first time I've had gummy shark this way. I wanted to include this recipe as it's a delicious addition to any repertoire. Thanks Mark, you're the, um, best.

INGREDIENTS

1 kg (2 lb 4 oz) gummy shark fillet (or skate works just as well)
100 g (⅓ cup) coarse sea salt
1 litre (4 cups) milk
6 garlic cloves, crushed with the blade of a knife, plus extra for rubbing the sourdough
4 fresh bay leaves
1 small bunch of thyme
300 g (10½ oz) waxy potatoes, such as Desiree or Dutch cream
200 ml (generous ¾ cup) extra virgin olive oil, plus extra for rubbing the sourdough
Freshly ground black pepper
Saltbush or sage leaves, deep-fried
Good sourdough bread

METHOD

Skin the fish, then rub with all of the salt, wrap in plastic wrap and refrigerate for 1 hour.

Rinse off excess salt under cold running water. Place the fish in a small saucepan, cover with the milk and add the crushed garlic, bay leaves and thyme. Bring to a gentle simmer and cook for 15 minutes until the fish starts to flake. Remove the fish and reserve the milk.

Place the potatoes in a saucepan, cover with water and bring to the boil. Reduce the heat and simmer until tender. Drain the potatoes and peel while hot.

Flake the fish into a heavy-based saucepan and place over low heat.

Push the potatoes and milky garlic through a ricer or sieve into the pan. Beat the fish and potatoes together with a wooden spoon, while alternately adding the reserved milk, then olive oil. Keep beating and adding a similar quantity of olive oil to milk. It should have the texture of mashed potato. Season with a good grind of black pepper.

Serve the brandade garnished with deep-fried saltbush or sage and grilled sourdough rubbed with garlic and olive oil.

RAW FISH

SERVES 2

This is an excellent dish to prepare when it's sweltering hot and you can't be arsed eating, let alone cooking anything.

INGREDIENTS

85 g (3 oz) white fish fillet (such as snapper, kingfish or cobia), trimmed, bloodline removed
Good pinch of sea salt
60 ml (¼ cup) lime juice
3 red Asian shallots, sliced
2 lemongrass stems, trimmed and finely sliced
1 handful each of mint and holy basil leaves, torn not chopped
5 bird's eye chillies, halved, seeded and sliced
2 tbsp fish sauce
2 tbsp coconut cream

METHOD

Slice the fillet in half lengthways down the centre, then slice it finely crossways – one serving should be about eight slices.

Combine the salt and lime juice in a bowl, add the fish, and mix well to marinate. Allow to stand for 3–4 minutes to cure.

Combine with the remaining ingredients and finish with the coconut cream. It should taste sour, salty and spicy. Adjust little by little as necessary, and serve.

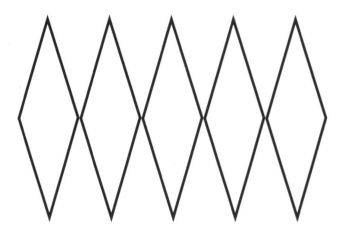

CALAMARI SAFARI

SERVES 2

This will feed two and is gluten-phobic, faulty stomach-friendly and safe for that irrepressible faux-vegetarian who is always ruining your dinner parties at the last minute – the pescatarian. It's probably Paleo-friendly too. We can't tell you if it is, but believe me, they'll tell you.

CALAMARI

2 fresh calamari tubes with tentacles, cleaned
Juice of 1 lemon
Sea salt

SEAWEED DRESSING

200 g (7 oz) fresh sea lettuce
2 French shallots, finely chopped
1 garlic clove, finely chopped
125 ml (½ cup) grapeseed oil
85 ml (⅓ cup) red wine vinegar – good quality,
    you cheap sods. No scrimping or using that old
    Cab Sav your misery wouldn't let you finish that
    night you were crying on the couch watching
    The Bodyguard for the millionth time
Olive oil, for frying
Lemon juice, for deglazing
1 bunch of leafage of your choice
Sea salt

METHOD

Split the calamari tubes in half. Flip them over and finely score without piercing the underside. (By score we mean that little crosshatch pattern you see at fancy pubs. You know the one, you salt'n'pepper fiend.) Set aside your fancy tubes.

Preheat the oven to 150°C (300°F) – don't fan force (or you'll spend a week peeling the sea lettuce off the walls of your oven).

Cook the sea lettuce for about 2 minutes until slightly crisp. The edges should be starting to lift and curl. Remove from the oven.

Sweat the shallots and garlic in the grapeseed oil. Pour the oil over the sea lettuce. Cover the bowl with plastic wrap and steep until cool.

Put into a blender (or Thermomix if you're not kicking it in the rungs of plebville) until blended. Add the red wine vinegar and a generous pinch of salt. Still better than a kale smoothie.

Get out your frying pan and add olive oil. Get that home skillet nice and hot – a cold pan means tough calamari. Fry both sides of the calamari for about 2–3 minutes until the calamari starts to caramelise. Deglaze the pan with lemon juice.

Remove the calamari from the pan and put on a tray or board.

Dress the leaves with pan juices and a touch of salt. Place on a plate to serve alongside. Drizzle your sea lettuce blend over the top of the calamari, Jackson Pollock style.

PICKLED MUSSELS AND CLAMS

★ ★ ★

SERVES 4

This is a brilliant snack with pre-dinner drinks. We are super lucky to have some excellent shellfish in Australia and this is a tasty way of showcasing that.

INGREDIENTS

250 g (9 oz) mussels, scrubbed and bearded
250 g (9 oz) clams
5 tbsp extra virgin olive oil
3 tbsp minced French shallot
2 tbsp minced carrot
1 tbsp minced garlic
60 ml (¼ cup) sherry vinegar
1 tsp finely chopped thyme
1 tsp chopped green olives
1 tsp finely chopped rosemary
¼ tsp smoked Spanish paprika
1 tsp finely chopped chillies
1 tsp marjoram
1 tsp finely grated lemon zest
1 tsp finely grated orange zest
1 tbsp chopped flat-leaf parsley
Sea salt

METHOD

In a large pot of boiling water, cook the mussels and clams for 20–30 seconds until they start to open. Using a slotted spoon, transfer the shellfish to a bowl. Remove the meat from their shells; discard any mussels or clams that do not open. Cover and refrigerate the mussels and clams. Strain the accumulated juices into a small bowl.

In a medium saucepan, heat the olive oil. Add the shallot, carrot and garlic and cook over a moderately low heat until softened. Add the shellfish juices and cook over moderate heat for about 4 minutes until reduced by half. Stir in the sherry vinegar, thyme, olives, rosemary, paprika, chilli, marjoram and lemon and orange zest and season with salt. Transfer this marinade to a bowl and refrigerate for about 30 minutes until cold.

Pour the marinade over the mussels and clams, cover and refrigerate for at least 3 hours and up to 8 hours. Spoon the mussels and clams into small bowls and top with parsley to serve.

★ ★ ★ ★ ★ ★ ★ ★ ★ ★ ★

NORTH AFRICAN FISH CURRY

SERVES 4

A light, floral and perfectly spiced curry.
The nutmeg gives this dish some serious back
palate, which works perfectly with the juices of
the seafood. Make sure the seafood is fresh as
fuck, though.

BAHARAT SPICE MIX

75 g (2½ oz) cumin seeds
75 g (2½ oz) coriander seeds
75 g (2½ oz) paprika
350 g (12 oz) ground cinnamon
1 tsp grated nutmeg
1 tsp whole cloves
1 tsp chilli flakes

CURRY

2 litres (8 cups) vegetable oil
2 onions, finely diced
6 garlic cloves, finely chopped
2 tbsp peeled and finely
   chopped fresh ginger
1 cup Baharat spice mix
1 kg (2 lb 4 oz) tomatoes, coarsely chopped
2 whole preserved lemons, roughly chopped
2 litres (8 cups) fish stock
250 g (9 oz) shelled prawns
1 kg (2 lb 4 oz) mussels, scrubbed and bearded
1 kg (2 lb 4 oz) clams
1 kg (2 lb 4 oz) fresh calamari, cleaned and cut into
   thin rounds (ask your fishmonger to clean for you)
10 sardine fillets
Sea salt and freshly ground black pepper
1 bunch of green leafage of your choice, to serve
Drizzle of olive oil

EQUIPMENT

Spice mill, coffee grinder or mortar and pestle
Cooking thermometer

METHOD

To make the spice mix, put all the spices in a dry
frying pan and toast until fragrant, then add to a
mortar and pestle, spice mill or coffee grinder and
grind to a fine powder.

Heat 1 litre (4 cups) of the vegetable oil in a frying
pan and fry the onion, garlic and ginger until the
onion just starts to brown. Remove from the pan.

Add the remaining vegetable oil to the pan, bring up
to about 180°C (356°F), checking the temperature
with a thermometer, then add 1 cup of the spices.
Fry all the spices for a couple of minutes until
fragrant, then add the cooked onion, tomatoes and
lemon to the pan.

Add the fish stock and bring to the boil. Simmer for
1½ hours, then check the seasoning.

Add the prawns, mussels, clams, calamari and
sardines and cook for 5 minutes. Serve straight
away with a side of green leaves and herbs and a
drizzle of olive oil.

BOQUERONES

SERVES 4

Anchovies are the best, so don't hesitate –
make these straight away because who doesn't
love anchovies? Boquerones are fillets of fresh
anchovies that have been marinated in vinegar,
olive oil, salt, garlic and parsley, just like in all the
tapas bars of Spain. According to *La Historia de la
Cocina Sefardí* (History of Sephardic Cuisine) by
Pepe Iglesias, anchovies in vinegar is a typical dish
of the Sephardic Jews, present in Spain until their
expulsion in the fifteenth century. The fact was that
it was necessary to preserve fish in the absence
of refrigeration to follow the religious precepts
of eating fish on Friday evening during Shabbat.
Drying and salting takes longer than the marinade
process, so *boquerones en vinagre* were born.

INGREDIENTS

500 g (1 lb 2 oz) very fresh boquerones
   (fresh uncured anchovies) (ask your fishmonger to
   clean the anchovies well by removing all bones,
   head, tail and spine)
500 ml (2 cups) white wine vinegar
125 ml (½ cup) extra virgin olive oil
2 garlic cloves, chopped
2 tbsp minced flat-leaf parsley
Sea salt

METHOD

Place the fish in a dish and cover with the vinegar.
Leave, covered, in the fridge for at least 6 hours.

Drain off the vinegar, then dress them with sea salt,
olive oil, the garlic and parsley. The boquerones can
be served immediately or can be stored, covered, in
the fridge for up to 3 days.

CLAMMA JAMMA

SERVES 4

More addictive than crack cocaine, eat this with flavour vehicles such as rice, noodles and bread. Don't eat while on crack cocaine. I use soumbala (locust bean) in this recipe, which is the go-to seasoning for all meats, vegetables and soups in West Africa. In the past, when there was nothing else to eat, soumbala was eaten with grains and provided essential nutrients. The locust bean tree, indigenous to West Africa, grows from Uganda north to Chad and west all the way to Senegal. These trees produce orange and red spherical flowers, which develop long pods, each containing up to 30 protein-rich seeds. One reason for the pods' appeal across West Africa may be the tree's resilience: it can withstand droughts and grows in pretty much all conditions. If you can't find soumbala, a good alternative is Korean black bean paste – something salty and funky will do just fine.

INGREDIENTS

3 tbsp soumbala
   (fermented locust bean paste)
1 tbsp mirin
2 garlic cloves, thinly sliced
2 dozen pipis or any small clams
125 ml (½ cup) cheap beer
2 spring onions (scallions), chopped
1 bunch of basil leaves

CHILLI OIL
(MAKES 375 ML/1½ CUPS)

100 g (3½ oz) dried red chillies
350 ml (scant 1½ cups) vegetable oil

METHOD

First make the chilli oil. In a food processor (or just with your knife on a cutting board), roughly chop the dried chillies. Toss them into a saucepan and toast them over medium–low heat, stirring constantly, until they become nose-burningly fragrant and the pan gets smoking hot – about 3–5 minutes. Be careful not to brown or burn the chillies.

Pour the vegetable oil over the chillies, then let the oil heat up until bubbles begin to form around the chillies – about 5 minutes. Remove the pan from the heat and let cool to room temperature. Store the chillies and oil in an airtight container, straining out the oil as needed. It should last for a couple weeks.

To make the clams, mix the soumbala with the mirin. Set aside.

Get a sauté pan hot and add 1 tablespoon of the chilli oil. Toss in the garlic and any larger clams that will take longer to cook. Cook, stirring, until the garlic is toasty and fragrant.

Add the remaining clams and douse with beer. Add the soumbala and mirin mixture and cover. Cook until almost all of the clams have opened, though it is better to leave a couple unopened than to overcook the whole batch.

Top the clams with a few tablespoons more of the chilli oil, the chopped spring onions and basil leaves. Serve immediately.

Leftover chilli oil can be stored in airtight containers and used for a variety of things, such as a base for salad dressings or a great finisher for your favourite pasta, though I wouldn't recommend it as a substitute for any water-based lubricants.

PRAWN JOLLOF

SERVES 6

A West African classic. Are the true origins Nigerian or Ghanaian? Who knows! Answers on a postcard, please. I cooked a version of this dish with weapon chef Paul Carmichael at Momofuku Seiōbo for an Afro-Caribbean collaboration dinner and I really enjoy how sophisticated and versatile jollof can actually be. This is definitely a recipe to follow to the tee as any substitutes or cowboy moves will only serve to denature the final dish.

INGREDIENTS

3 garlic bulbs, peeled
2 tsp sea salt
2 medium–large onions, finely sliced
4 red capsicums (peppers), trimmed and
   finely sliced
60 ml (¼ cup) sunflower oil
6 large shell-on prawns, peeled and heads reserved
½ Scotch bonnet pepper, seeded and sliced
115 g (4 oz) plum tomatoes, diced
1 tsp dried thyme
½ tsp ground ginger
½ tsp cayenne pepper or alternative
¼ tsp smoked Spanish paprika
1 heaped tsp tomato paste (concentrated purée)
525 ml (generous 2 cups) hot chicken stock
1 tsp red pepper or chilli oil
250 g (1¼ cups) white basmati rice

METHOD

Make a paste out of the garlic and 1 teaspoon of the salt.

Soften the onions and capsicums in the sunflower oil over high heat for 5 minutes, stirring frequently. Add the garlic paste, prawn heads, Scotch bonnet pepper, tomatoes and dry seasonings and cook for another 10 minutes over medium heat, stirring frequently. Add the tomato paste and prawn meat and cook for another minute or so, then remove from the heat and take out the prawn heads. Set heads aside for serving.

Blend the mixture in a blender with 200 ml (generous ¾ cup) of the chicken stock (if you have prepared this in advance, reheat it first). Add another 200 ml (¾ cup) of the stock and blend until the mixture is smooth.

Add the pepper oil and final teaspoon of salt, then pour (2½ cups) of this mixture back into the pan. Heat the sauce until it is lightly bubbling.

Measure out your rice, then add to the pan. The pan should have a tight-fitting lid, but if it doesn't you can use some foil with the shiny side facing down to retain the heat. Stir gently so that all the rice is coated with the red sauce, then reduce the heat to a very low flame – the lowest possible.

Cover and simmer for 10 minutes. Open the lid and stir gently again. It is important to get under the centre of the pan so all the rice cooks at the same rate. Cover and simmer for another 10 minutes. Open and stir for a final time, then simmer for a final 10 minutes. This makes 30 minutes cooking time in total. Turn the heat off and allow to steam, covered, for another 15 minutes.

Open the lid and leave to stand for 5 minutes, uncovered. Fluff with a fork to separate the rice, slowly working inwards from the edge of the pan in a swirling motion. If the rice is not completely cooked, add the remaining stock, stir gently, then place back over low heat for another 10 minutes. Spoon the rice out onto a separate dish, decorate with the prawn heads and serve. Goes great with the Braised green beans and samphire (page 134). You can also serve with a salmon skin cracker as pictured – good luck sourcing it.

SARDINES AND CHERMOULA

★ ★ ★

SERVES 6

This was one of the first dishes at Africola mark 2. We are lucky to have some of the finest sardines in the world, which come straight out of Port Lincoln in South Australia. This is pretty much the only way I eat sardines because it's a perfectly balanced dish. Salty, tangy, spicy and garlicky and any other adjectives that you can put a 'y' behind.

INGREDIENTS

6 whole sardines, cleaned and butterflied
1 lemon, halved

GREEN CHERMOULA

12 anchovy fillets, salt-packed,
  rinsed and patted dry
5 garlic cloves
50 g (2 oz) bird's eye chillies
2 tbsp capers, drained
Pinch of sea salt
½ tsp ground cumin
½ tsp freshly ground black pepper
1 tsp lemon juice
100 g (2 cups) chopped coriander (cilantro)
100 g (3½ cups) chopped flat-leaf parsley
100 ml (scant ½ cup) olive oil
1 tbsp diced preserved lemon rind
2 finger limes or flesh of 1 lime

EQUIPMENT

Charcoal barbecue or hot skillet

METHOD

To make the chermoula, pound the ingredients in the order opposite using a mortar and pestle. Pound each one to a coarse paste before adding the next. Pour in the olive oil at the end, then stir in the preserved lemon and finger limes.

Marinate the sardines for 30 minutes in enough chermoula to cover them.

Get a charcoal fire ready. Wait for the coals to ash over before cooking and place the sardines on a wire grilling rack. When I make this, I keep the fish close to, even touching, the embers. I look for the skin to darken and blister after a few minutes on each side, depending on the embers' heat. Once the skin looks right, the fish should be cooked inside. Alternatively, you can cook the sardines in a hot skillet on the stove.

Grill the lemon halves face down to bring out their sweetness and serve with the sardines.

Serve with more chermoula spooned over the top.

★ ★ ★ ★ ★ ★ ★ ★ ★ ★

CHARDONNAY ROLLMOPS

MAKES 6 ROLLMOPS

A fresh take on my childhood favourite. I ate so many of these as a child I cannot stomach them if they are made with spirit vinegar, hence the lighter style found in this recipe.

INGREDIENTS

6 large fresh herrings, descaled, gutted and filleted
90 g (⅔ cup) sea salt

MARINADE

500 ml (2 cups) Chardonnay vinegar
250 ml (1 cup) Chardonnay
12 juniper berries
12 Kampot peppercorns
3 bay leaves
1 tbsp light brown sugar
1 tsp caraway seeds
Zest of 1 large orange, pared into wide strips
    with no white pith
1 small red or white onion, very thinly sliced

EQUIPMENT

3 x 500 ml (17 fl oz) sterilised preserving jars

METHOD

Check the herring fillets for any pin bones and remove as necessary. Dissolve the salt in 500 ml (2 cups) cold water to make a brine, then add the fillets. Leave for 2–3 hours.

Meanwhile, make the marinade. Put all the ingredients in a saucepan, bring slowly to the boil and simmer for a minute. Set aside to cool.

Drain the herring fillets from the brine and pat them dry with paper towel. Roll them up, skin-side out, from tail end to head end, and pack the rolls into three sterilised preserving jars.

Pour the marinade over the herrings, making sure you get some of the spices and zest in each jar, then seal.

Store in the fridge for at least 3 days before eating. They're best eaten 5–10 days from jarring, but will keep for up to a month. The longer you leave them, the softer and more pickled they'll get.

I became vegan for two reasons: the first was to get over the mass consumption of Christmas and the other was to better understand cooking without any animal products.

Are you tired of meat? No. Would you die without cheese? Obviously, yes, because you're a human with a pulse and needs, damn it. Great. Now go out and become a vegan for a month. I've just come off riding a 730.001-hour long wave (not that I'm counting) of zero animal products in or around my mouth. And I decided I'd ice the cake with 31 days of zero alcohol too. In the realm of hospitality, giving up alcohol AND animal products simultaneously is not far off announcing you're moving to the Antarctic with no-one for company but the corpse of your favourite aunt and an elaborate hat.

Teetering on the precipice of Stalin-esque paranoia, knowing my mates would do something to fuck up my self discipline, I swore I'd do my best to keep my new 'lifestyle choice' off YouTube first and out of the lives of others second. No. The words fling themselves out of your mouth. You've turned into a social kamikaze before you realise it: 'Would you like some steak?' 'I'm a vegan'; 'Want to come to my fire-pit party and sacrifice prosperity goats?' 'I would, but I'm a vegan'; 'SOMEBODY HELP! MY SON IS BEING MAULED BY A SEAL DRESSED AS A SHARK!' 'I can't, I'm a vegan.'

You are so worn down by constantly saying no that hyper-morality becomes your sanity's last bastion. You might be eating the double-cream brie, but at least you aren't contributing to the evils of mass consumption. Until you realise that you still are. I found myself regularly on the hunt for substitutes. Effectively, your stance against industrial-scale farming is severely undercut by your purchase of chemical-packed alternatives. It highlighted the point for me that it isn't the use of animals that's the issue, but the complete disregard for everything consumable on an industrial scale.

After the fifth day, my body had betrayed me and decided it really enjoyed being vegan. I woke up hangover free for the first time since birth, and dropped 7 kg. It's almost as if I was murdered and replaced by some green fundamentalist. Still, it's slightly creepy when someone you know behaves atypically; it's borderline terrifying when the person behaving out of character is wearing your shoes and your haircut and looks like you and is you. I actually enjoyed cooking without animal products and having to really think about food again, exploring other food cultures and alternative ingredients. I think everyone should go vegan for a month. It's great for the body, the mind, the environment, and it turns fundamentalist vegan bullies into more of a frenzied flesh puppet jerked around by uncontrollable opportunism. Go vegan for a while and you will appreciate meat a lot more. Who would have thought?

03

V *is for* VEGETABLES

VEGETABLES ARE THE MOST PROMINENT FIXTURE ON OUR
MENU AND MAKE UP THREE-QUARTERS OF OUR DAILY DISHES.
MORE RESTAURANTS SHOULD HAVE A MENU THAT LEANS TOWARDS
VEGETABLES AND GRAINS SO WE MIGHT HAVE A FIGHTING CHANCE
TO TURN OUR CURRENT CLIMATE CHANGE WORRIES AROUND.
THE RECIPES HERE RANGE FROM COMPLICATED TO DEAD
EASY AND ARE SUPER FUCKING YUM.

WHOLE ROAST CAULIFLOWER WITH FIG AND PISTACHIO AGRODOLCE AND TAHINI SAUCE

★ ★ ★

SERVES 4

One of Africola's classic dishes. This was the first version of the dish and it is way too delicious to discard it.

INGREDIENTS

1 large cauliflower
2½ tbsp extra virgin olive oil
100 g (⅓ cup) unsalted butter
50 g (2 oz) ground turmeric
1 garlic clove, crushed
Juice of 1 lemon
100 g (3½ oz) Fig and pistachio agrodolce (page 200)
Sea salt and freshly ground white pepper

TAHINI SAUCE

200 g (¾ cup) tahini
3 garlic cloves
80 ml (⅓ cup) lemon juice, or more to taste
¼ tsp sea salt, or more to taste
Freshly ground white pepper

METHOD

Start with the tahini sauce. Add the tahini, 100 ml (scant ½ cup) lukewarm water, the garlic, lemon juice, salt and pepper to a food processor or blender and blend together until the sauce is creamy and emulsified.

If the mixture is too thick, slowly add more water until it reaches the preferred consistency. You may need quite a bit of water depending on the thickness of your tahini. I add heaps more lemon juice because I love how the acid cuts through the richness of this dish.

Now blanch the cauliflower for 10 minutes in salted boiling water and then refresh it in ice water.

Add the olive oil to a hot roasting tin and roast the hell out of the cauliflower for about 30 minutes until it starts to caramelise. Once all browned, add the butter to the tin and, when it's foaming, add the turmeric and garlic. Baste the cauli with the turmeric butter until it has stained the cauliflower, then return to the oven to cook for another 10 minutes.

Drain the cauliflower and season with salt and white pepper and a squeeze of lemon juice. Place the tahini on the base of a plate with the cauliflower on top of that and serve with the agrodolce drizzled over. BOOM!!

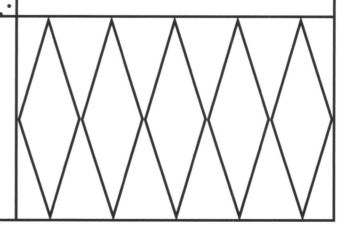

ISBN: 978-1-76-052386-2

LEEK VINAIGRETTE

SERVES 2

This classic bistro dish reminds me of my time in London, in the basement of the first French kitchen I ever worked at. The smell of the capers and mustard, the steam from the poaching water forming sweat beads on the dirty walls, the paper towel all over the benches to drain the leeks. This dish taught me about simplicity and balance; it also taught me about versatility. A dish like this can sit alongside freshly hot-smoked salmon, a slow-cooked rib of aged beef with that caramelised yellow fat or with soft-boiled quails' eggs and garlic croutons. The options are endless.

INGREDIENTS

3–4 small leeks, white and light green parts only, washed well
60 ml (¼ cup) Champagne vinegar
½ tsp sea salt
⅛ tsp freshly ground black pepper
1 tbsp minced French shallots
1 tbsp minced capers
1 tsp Dijon mustard
1 tsp wholegrain mustard
220 ml (scant 1 cup) vegetable oil

METHOD

Bring a large pot of water to the boil and salt it. Add the leeks and cook until soft, about 15 minutes. To test for doneness, insert a paring knife into one of the leeks – it should be able to go through the leek with barely any resistance. Transfer the leeks to a plate and set them aside to cool to room temperature.

In a medium bowl, whisk together the vinegar, salt, pepper, shallots, capers and mustard. Once amalgamated, start adding the oil in a slow, steady stream, whisking constantly to create a smooth, even vinaigrette. Set aside.

Cut each leek in half lengthways, then cut the halves in half crossways. Place on a platter or individual plates, cut-side up, and cover with the sauce. Let the leeks sit for at least 10 minutes before serving so that the sauce has a chance to work its way between the leeks' layers.

SMASHED CUCUMBER SALAD WITH TOASTED CHILLI OIL

SERVES 2

One of the best salads around. Don't be mean with the Sichuan oil though – the labneh will take a lot of the spice, so you're left with that gentle numbing on your tongue.

INGREDIENTS

1 large cucumber or 2 Lebanese (short) cucumbers
   (about 300 g/10½ oz)
2 tsp finely chopped pickled chillies
2 small garlic cloves, finely chopped
60 ml (¼ cup) clear rice vinegar, or to taste
Pinch of sugar
1 tbsp Sichuan chilli oil
1 tsp sesame oil
2 tsp labneh or 6 tbsp Greek yoghurt,
   drained of excess moisture
1 tsp toasted black and white sesame seeds
Sea salt

METHOD

Place the cucumber on a chopping board and whack it gently with a cleaver a few times until it splinters and opens up with jagged edges. Cut it into bite-sized pieces and place in a bowl. Sprinkle with ½ teaspoon sea salt and leave for 15–20 minutes, then drain and place the cucumber in a bowl.

For the dressing, put the chillies, garlic, vinegar, sugar and a pinch of salt in a small bowl. Stir in the chilli and sesame oils and the labneh.

To serve, pour the dressing over the cucumber and garnish with the sesame seeds.

BRAISED WHITE PEAS, CURED EGG YOLK AND PRESERVED LEMON

SERVES 4

An excellent vegetarian main served with spiced yoghurt and flat breads, this can also sit alongside roast chicken or slow-cooked lamb.

INGREDIENTS

250 g (2 cups) dried white peas (safed matar)
3 tbsp Greek yoghurt
125 g (4½ oz) tinned chopped tomatoes
1 tsp amchur (tangy dried mango powder)
3 Indian bay leaves (leave out if you do not have these)
125 ml (½ cup) Africola cure-all tahini sauce (page 195)
½ preserved lemon, finely diced
Coriander (cilantro) leaves

CURED EGG YOLK

2 egg yolks
100 g (scant ½ cup) sugar
100 g (⅓ cup) table salt

CHOLAY SPICE MIX

3 tsp ground cumin
2 tsp ground coriander
½ tsp fenugreek powder
½ tsp ground ginger
¾ tsp ground cinnamon
¾ tsp ground cloves
¾ tsp freshly ground black pepper
¾ tsp ground cardamom
½ tsp ajwain
1 tsp ground fennel seeds

MASALA

65 g (¼ cup) ghee
¼ tsp cumin seeds
¼ tsp fenugreek seeds
250 g (9 oz) finely minced onion
¾ tsp sea salt
½ tsp cayenne pepper
10 garlic cloves, minced
1 tbsp peeled and finely chopped fresh ginger

METHOD

To make the cured egg yolk, place the yolks in the sugar and salt mix, cover and freeze for 48 hours. Gently wash in cold water and set aside.

Soak the dried white peas in 1.5 litres (6 cups) water overnight.

Cook the soaked white peas in plenty of water until soft. This can take an hour or more, but watch the peas as the degree of 'driedness' will impact the cooking time.

Make the cholay spice mix. Grind any spices that you have as whole spices to form powders, then mix everything together.

To prepare the masala, heat the ghee in a sauté pan. Add the cumin seeds and sauté until they start to brown, then add the fenugreek and sauté for about 1 minute until they also begin to brown. Next, add the onion with the salt and cayenne. Sauté these until the water evaporates and the onion turns brown. Now add the garlic and ginger, mix with the onion and cook for 2 minutes.

Add 3½ tablespoons of the cholay spice mix and sauté for 1 minute. Add the yoghurt, 1 tablespoon at a time, until almost all of the moisture is gone. This forms a spice paste.

Add the tomatoes, amchur and bay leaves, if using. Cook for about 5 minutes until the tomatoes begin to soften.

Now, add the cooked white peas to this spice paste, with enough of the cooking water to form a nice gravy from the spice paste. The white peas will be just submerged in the gravy. Add more water if the cooking water is not enough.

Spread the tahini sauce on the base of a large plate. Spoon the peas on top, cover with the preserved lemon and, with a fine grater or Microplane, grate the cured egg yolks over the peas. Sprinkle over the coriander.

COS HEARTS AND GREEN GODDESS DRESSING

SERVES 2

This salad is bullshit easy. It can be whipped up in less than 10 minutes and be on the table before the parmesan hits the spaghetti sauce. You're welcome.

INGREDIENTS

½ avocado
2 tablespoons mayonnaise
2 tablespoons chopped chervil, plus 5 g
  (¼ cup) whole leaves
1 tablespoon chopped chives
1 small French shallot, chopped
1 tablespoon extra virgin olive oil
2 baby cos lettuce hearts
Sea salt and freshly ground black pepper

METHOD

Blend or process the avocado, mayonnaise, chervil, chives, shallot, 60 ml (¼ cup) water and the extra virgin olive oil until smooth, then season to taste.

Quarter the lettuce hearts lengthways, arrange on a platter, then drizzle with the dressing. Scatter with the extra chervil leaves.

THE WORLD'S GREATEST
ROAST POTATOES FOR TOTAL IDIOTS

SERVES 4

As it says on the packet – you can't fuck this one up. If you do, please tag me in all the photos.

INGREDIENTS

1.5 kg (3 lb 5 oz) good roasting potatoes with little starch, like Diane, or large Kipfler potatoes, peeled, cut in half and washed until the excess starch is rinsed off and the water is clear
200 g (7 oz) rendered pork fat or lard
50 g (2 oz) paprika
5 sprigs of thyme, leaves picked
10 garlic cloves, crushed in their skins
Sea salt and freshly ground black pepper

METHOD

Preheat the oven to 200°C (400°F).

Boil the potatoes for 10 minutes or until just soft.

Add the fat to a hot heavy-based saucepan and heat over high, then add the potatoes flat-side down. DON'T BURN YOURSELF OR SET FIRE TO YOUR HOUSE. Get a crispy golden colour on all sides. Once all crispy, transfer the potatoes to a baking tray.

Drizzle with a little of the warmed fat and sprinkle with the paprika, thyme leaves, garlic, sea salt and black pepper.

Roast for 20 minutes, tossing occasionally until they are super crispy and dried out a little. The centre will be like mash potato and pretty much the best vehicle ever for all kinds of sauces, gravies, meat juices, whatever – all of it.

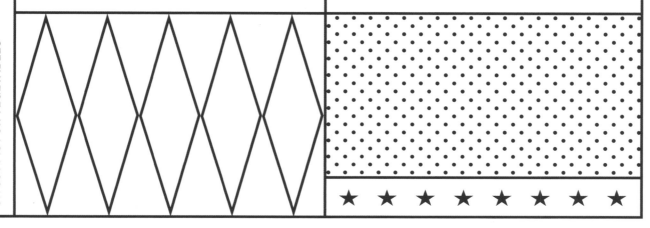

DAHL WITH SPICED BUTTER

SERVES 4

This is probably one of the few 'authentic' dishes in this book. It's terribly romantic and transports you to India in a heartbeat, so fucking around with it wouldn't do it any justice. I personally prefer tempering the ghee with the charcoal as it adds a smoky flavour and also looks badass to your mates, especially when they think all they will be eating is some hippy pot-luck dish.

INGREDIENTS

250 g (9 oz) split pigeon pea lentils
1 onion, chopped
2 tomatoes, chopped
1–2 green chillies, chopped or slit lengthways
1 cm (½ inch) piece of fresh ginger, peeled and
  finely chopped or grated
1 tsp ground turmeric
Pinch of asafoetida
1–2 tbsp thick (double) cream
1–2 pinches of garam masala
1 tsp crushed dried fenugreek leaves (kasuri methi)
1 tbsp chopped coriander (cilantro) leaves,
  plus extra to serve
Sea salt
Green mango atchar, to serve

DHUNGAR METHOD (OPTIONAL)

¼ tsp ghee or oil

TEMPERING

1–2 tbsp butter or ghee or 2 tbsp oil
1 tsp cumin seeds
2–3 dried red chillies
Generous pinch of asafoetida
5–6 garlic cloves, finely chopped
½ tsp red chilli powder

EQUIPMENT (OPTIONAL)
for the dhungar method

Small piece of charcoal (please use natural charcoal)
Small steel bowl

METHOD

To prepare the lentils, rinse and add them to a pot with the onion, tomato, green chilli and ginger, then add about 1 litre (4 cups) water. Add the turmeric and asafoetida and stir well.

Cook the lentils for about 1 hour in the simmering water until they become soft and creamy. Mash the dahl with a wired whisk or spoon – if the dahl looks thick, add some more water to get a medium consistency. Simmer the dahl for 3–4 more minutes after mashing.

Once the desired consistency has been reached, add the cream, garam masala, fenugreek and coriander leaves and salt. Switch off the heat and mix well. Check the salt before you add the tempering.

Next is the dhungar method of flavouring the dahl with the smoky fumes of burnt charcoal; if you are doing this. With the help of tongs, burn the charcoal till it becomes red hot. Place the red hot charcoal in a small steel bowl. Pour the oil or ghee on the charcoal. You will see fumes emanating as soon as you pour the oil or ghee over. Place this bowl on the dahl. Cover the pot with a lid and let the dahl infuse with the charcoal fumes for a minute – the longer you leave the smoking bowl in the dahl, the smokier the flavour. Remove the bowl carefully with the help of tongs and cover the dahl.

To prepare the tempering, heat the butter, ghee or oil in a small pan. Add the cumin seeds and crackle them. Now, add the red chilli, asafoetida and chopped garlic. Let the garlic brown and the red chilli change colour. Make sure to fry the tempering ingredients over a low heat so that you don't burn them. Lastly, add the red chilli powder. Stir and switch off the heat. Pour all the butter into the dahl.

Serve the dahl with lots of coriander and the green mango atchar.

HOT-AND-SOUR EGGPLANT

SERVES 4

This dish is super moreish, very rich and does completely take over the palate, however you will find you keep going back for more. Just be careful of the sauce on your hands as it does resemble molten lava.

INGREDIENTS

300 g (2 cups) '00' flour
300 g (scant 2½ cups) cornflour
Vegetable oil, for frying
2–3 eggplants (aubergines), cut lengthways into 3 cm (1¼ inch) wide slices
1 onion, sliced 1 cm (½ inch)
250 g (1 cup) butter
10 basil leaves, torn
Fried garlic (page 203), to serve

HOT·AND·SOUR SAUCE

2 tbsp olive oil
1 red onion, minced
1 white onion, minced
4 Calabrian chillies, minced
2 garlic cloves, minced
1 tsp hot pepper flakes
1 tbsp salt
500 ml (2 cups) white wine vinegar
500 g (2¼ cups) sugar

METHOD

Prepare the sauce. Heat a large saucepan over medium heat and coat with the olive oil. Sweat the onions, chilli and garlic for about 5–7 minutes until the onions soften and become translucent. Add the hot pepper flakes, salt, vinegar, sugar and 1 litre (4 cups) water and cook over medium heat for about 1 hour until the liquid is reduced by three-quarters to a syrup-like consistency. Remove from the heat and reserve.

Make the eggplant. Sift together the flour and cornflour. Fill a deep pot halfway up with oil and heat it to 190°C (375°F) over medium–high heat.

Dredge the eggplant and onion in the flour-cornflour mixture, shake off the excess, and fry for 4–5 minutes until golden. Work in batches as necessary so as not to crowd the pot.

While the eggplant and onion are frying, warm the sauce and butter together in a saucepan.

Once the eggplant and onion are cooked, drain well, and transfer to a bowl. Pour the sauce over the fried vegetables and toss very gently to coat. Transfer to a plate and garnish with basil leaves and fried garlic.

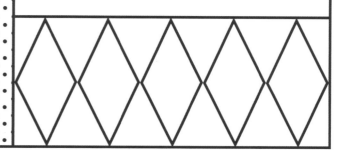

KOHLRABI AND SEAWEED

SERVES 4

This little dish has it all – sweetness from the apple juice, earthiness from the kohlrabi and that super savoury characteristic from the seaweed, all brought together by the butter, which helps all those flavours coat the palate. To turn this vegan, use a tablespoon or two of Nuttelex instead of the butter as you need that fat content for the mouthfeel. Substitute the honey for maple syrup and shazam! Those vegan pot-luck dinners will never be the same.

INGREDIENTS

250 ml (1 cup) apple juice
1 tbsp Maggi seasoning
100 g (3½ oz) fresh sea lettuce
1 sheet of toasted nori
1 sheet of kombu
1–2 tbsp butter
2 kohlrahbi, peeled and sliced into 6
Large pinch of sea salt
80 g (3 oz) unsalted butter
1 tsp local honey

METHOD

Heat the apple juice, Maggi, sea lettuce, nori and kombu together over your stove's lowest heat for 2 minutes. If you've got 20–40 minutes, let the seaweed steep in the juice off the heat.

Melt the butter in a large pan over medium heat. Once the butter foam subsides, add the kohlrabi and a large pinch of salt. Toss once to coat the kohlrabi in the butter and add the apple juice, discarding the kombu.

Cover the pan and cook, shaking it or opening the lid to stir the kohlrabi occasionally. Gauge the doneness of the kohlrabi after 6 or 7 minutes and cook them to your taste – al dente or soft. Add the honey and serve.

HAND-FORAGED SUMMER VEG AND 'NDUJA DRESSING

SERVES 4

Foraging in your garden is way cooler sounding than gardening in your garden. It makes you seem more in tune with mother nature, at one with the earth, European even. If you think like me that foraging in your garden is awesome, wait till you forage in the aisles of your local supermarket for those seasonal vegetables. Wholesome bliss.

INGREDIENTS

500 g (1lb 2 oz) 'nduja (whole not jarred)
100 ml (scant ½ cup) light soy sauce
100 ml (scant ½ cup) white balsamic vinegar
1 kg (2 lb 4 oz) seasonal vegetables, trimmed
    however you like

METHOD

Break the 'nduja up in a pan. Stir until dissolved.

Take off the heat. Add the soy and vinegar and stir until the sauce comes together. Pour the sauce into a bowl and serve with the raw young veg.

BEETROOT AND YOGHURT

SERVES 4

Another addition to the bullshit easy salad collection. Everyone buys beetroot at the farmers' market, but I bet most leave it to be fossilised in the vegetable drawer at the bottom of their fridge. This recipe basically cuts to the front of the queue when you're trying to figure out WTF to do with it. If you have any leftover baked beetroot, place in a container, cover with good olive oil, a pinch of juniper, a sprig of rosemary, some crushed garlic and freshly ground black pepper. It will keep as long as it's covered with the oil for at least 6 months in the fridge.

INGREDIENTS

1 bunch of beetroot
1 kg (2 lb 4 oz) of the best yoghurt you can afford
2 garlic cloves, crushed
125 ml (½ cup) olive oil
2 tbsp lemon juice
100 g (2 cups) finely chopped mint
¼ tsp chopped fresh habanero or bird's eye chilli
Sea salt and freshly ground black pepper

EQUIPMENT

Dehydrator (optional)

METHOD

Steam the beetroot for 1 hour, then peel the skin when they are cool enough to handle. Cut into about 5 mm (¼ inch) thick slices and place in a dehydrator or low oven until semi-dried – about 2 hours.

Drain the yoghurt and season with salt and pepper and the garlic. Place the yoghurt on a plate with the beets on top.

Mix the olive oil, lemon juice, mint, chilli and some seasoning together to make the dressing, then garnish the yoghurt and beetroot with the dressing.

VEGAN MAPO TOFU

SERVES 4

One of the most satisfying vegan comfort dishes of all time. Inspired by Shannon Martinez, who is the most accomplished vegan chef in the world today or ever for that matter. This isn't hyperbole, it's fact. Her vegan food hacks of our favourite home classics are genius, and I recommend everyone buy her cookbooks, obviously after buying my book of course. Make heaps, invite some friends over and don't leave the couch for days.

INGREDIENTS

500 ml (2 cups) boiling water
2 tsp vegan chicken stock powder
1 tsp mushroom powder (optional)
1 tsp MSG (aka secret ingredient, gold dust, your sous chef)
100 g (1 cup) TVP (textured vegetable protein) mince
500 g (1 lb 2 oz) fresh firm tofu, cut into 2.5 cm (1 inch) cubes
2 tbsp dry white wine
60 ml (¼ cup) Sichuan chilli oil
2 tsp coarsely ground Sichuan pepper
6 garlic cloves, peeled and smashed
2 tbsp doubanjiang (spicy fermented bean paste)
2 tbsp chopped Thai chillies
½ tsp vegan fish sauce
2 tbsp demerara sugar
2 tbsp soy sauce
3 tbsp cornflour
2 tbsp chopped Chinese chives, for garnish
2 tbsp chopped spring onions (scallions), for garnish
Rice, to serve

GARLIC AND BLACK BEAN SAUCE

2 tbsp vegetable oil
1 tbsp fermented black bean sauce
1 tbsp minced garlic
1 tsp vegan fish sauce

CRISP CHILLIES

Coconut oil
10 sun-dried curd chillies or other good-quality dried chillies

METHOD

To prepare the garlic and black bean sauce, heat a wok or sauté pan over high heat and add the oil. Once that's smoking hot, add the black bean sauce, garlic and vegan fish sauce. Take off the heat and stir until combined.

Pour the boiling water into a large bowl. Add the stock powder, mushroom powder, if using, MSG and mince. Leave until cool or until the mince is hydrated. Separate the mince and the liquid and set aside.

Now make the crisp chillies. Heat a wok or sauté pan over medium–high heat and add a slick of coconut oil. Add the dried chillies and fry until a dark red, about 3 minutes. Let cool, then grind in a spice grinder.

Put a large pot of salted water on to boil. Blanch the tofu cubes for 4–5 minutes just to warm them through and firm them up a bit. Drain and set aside.

In the same pan used for the chillies, over medium heat, add 2 tablespoons of the TVP stock liquid and 1 tablespoon of the white wine to deglaze, scraping up all the brown bits. Dump the liquid into the bowl with the mince.

Heat 2 tablespoons of the chilli oil in the same pan over medium heat. Add 1 tablespoon of the garlic and black bean sauce, the Sichuan pepper, garlic, doubanjiang and crisp chillies. Cook for 3–5 minutes, adding the remaining TVP chicken stock and wine in splashes to deglaze the pan as needed.

Add the mince and juices to the pan, along with the Thai chillies and fish sauce. Turn up the heat to high. Add the reserved tofu and gently fold into the mix, trying to keep the cubes as intact as possible. Once the mixture is bubbling, turn the heat down to a simmer and add the sugar and soy sauce. Taste it; you want the sugar to balance out the heat and savouriness. Add more if needed.

While the mixture is still bubbling, make a cornflour slurry: whisk together the cornflour with 3 tablespoons cold water in a small bowl. Add the slurry to the pan and stir to combine. Take off the heat and add the remaining chilli oil. Garnish with heaps of Chinese chives and spring onions, and serve with rice.

EASY-PEASY GREENS AKA MOROGO

SERVES 4

Morogo is the Tswana word for 'vegetables' and is the name for a wild leafy African spinach. In this recipe we are using kale because it's wildly available. If you can't find any kale, use large-leaf spinach.

INGREDIENTS

1 garlic clove
1 long red chilli, finely chopped
2½ tbsp extra virgin olive oil
400 g (14 oz) tin chickpeas
350 g (12 oz) kale
2½ tbsp filtered water
200 ml (generous ¾ cup) Sheba (page 142)
80 ml (⅓ cup) Hellfire oil (page 193)
Sea salt

METHOD

Bruise the garlic with a pinch of salt using a mortar and pestle, then pound into small pieces with the chilli, but not to a paste.

Transfer to a hot frying pan with the olive oil and sweat it until the garlic is fragrant and translucent, then add the chickpeas and cook for 2 minutes.

Add the kale and the water and cook until the kale has wilted. Add the sheba and cook for a further 5 minutes.

Serve on a large plate and drizzle over the hellfire oil to finish.

PARSNIPS AND BUTTERMILK

SERVES 4

The buttermilk in this recipe is a little nod to the 'Beach Jesus' of Australian cuisine, David Moyle. A man so good looking he makes me look like the face from a pamphlet about diabetes. Moyle loves only three things in life: saltbush, buttermilk and putting both those things on skewers. Thank you for the inspiration, mate xxx

INGREDIENTS

100 g (⅓ cup) unsalted butter
60 ml (¼ cup) olive oil
2 onions, thinly sliced
2 tbsp biryani spice mix
1 garlic clove, chopped
500 ml (2 cups) vegetable stock
4 cardamom pods
3 star anise
600 ml (2⅓ cups) buttermilk
50 g (⅓ cup) plain flour
1 kg (2 lb 4 oz) parsnips, peeled and
   halved lengthways
115 g (⅓ cup) honey
2 large sprigs of rosemary
Sea salt and freshly ground black pepper

METHOD

Heat half the butter and 2 tablespoons of the oil in a large saucepan over medium–low heat. Add the onion and 1 teaspoon salt and cook, stirring, for about 15 minutes or until caramelised and golden. Add the spice mix and garlic and cook, stirring, for about 2–3 minutes until fragrant. Add the stock, cardamom and star anise and increase the heat to medium. Simmer for 15 minutes or until reduced by half.

Whisk the buttermilk and flour together in a bowl. Strain the onion mixture, discarding the solids. Return the liquid to a clean saucepan and place over low heat. Whisk in the buttermilk mixture and cook, stirring constantly, for 20 minutes or until thickened. Season to taste and set aside.

Preheat the oven to 180°C (350°F).

Melt the remaining butter and oil in an ovenproof frying pan over medium heat. Add the parsnips, cut-side down, and cook for 5 minutes or until golden. Turn and cook for a further 2 minutes or until golden. Pour the honey over the parsnips and add the rosemary to the pan. Transfer to the oven and cook for a further 15 minutes or until cooked through.

Gently reheat the buttermilk sauce. Spoon onto a plate and top with parsnips. Drizzle over any remaining pan juices and rosemary. Serve with Pap (page 142).

CHARCOAL CARROTS AND STEAKHOUSE DRESSING

SERVES 4

This dish is like white trash crudités, but by God it's delicious.

CARROTS

1 kg (2 lb 4 oz) carrots, trimmed and
  sliced lengthways
2 tbsp extra virgin olive oil
Sea salt and freshly ground black pepper
Chilli sauce, to serve (optional)

BARBECUE SAUCE

1 small onion, diced
2 tsp minced garlic
250 ml (1 cup) orange juice
60 ml (¼ cup) balsamic vinegar
60 ml (¼ cup) sherry vinegar
100 ml (scant ½ cup) soy sauce
200 g (scant 1 cup) ketchup
60 ml (¼ cup) honey
1 tbsp Tabasco sauce
1 tbsp cumin seeds, toasted
1 cinnamon stick, toasted
2 tbsp brown sugar
1 tsp dried sage
¼ tsp dried thyme
1 tbsp tomato paste (concentrated purée)
175 g (½ cup) molasses

STEAKHOUSE DRESSING

1½ tbsp dried parsley
½ tsp dried dill
½ tsp garlic powder
½ tsp onion powder
¼ tsp freshly ground black pepper
¼ tsp dried chives
¼ tsp sea salt
⅛ tsp cayenne pepper
65 g (¼ cup) mayonnaise
60 ml (¼ cup) buttermilk

METHOD

First prepare the barbecue sauce. In a large frying pan over medium heat, sweat the onion and garlic for about 6 minutes until the onion is translucent. Add the rest of the ingredients and simmer for about 30 minutes over low heat until the sauce has thickened. Transfer to a bowl.

Now prepare the dressing. Mix the spices together with the mayonnaise and buttermilk.

Preheat the oven to 170°C (325°F).

Toss the carrots with salt, pepper, olive oil and a good splash of barbecue sauce.

Grill the carrots over charcoal or on a hot griddle, basting with the barbecue sauce until they acquire a nice char. Be sure not to burn the carrots, just give them some colour. Transfer to a parchment-lined baking sheet and roast in the oven for 15 minutes until tender. Serve on a platter with heaps of the dressing and a side of chilli sauce, if you're that way inclined.

The barbecue sauce will keep for up to 1 month in an airtight container.

BRAISED GREEN BEANS AND SAMPHIRE

SERVES 4

This dish is one of my go-tos for a perfect side for lamb or any grilled fish. It's slightly briny and super savoury. Make a bunch and keep it in the fridge for a cold pick-me-up when snacking.

INGREDIENTS

2 onions, chopped
2 garlic cloves, chopped
125 ml (½ cup) extra virgin olive oil
500 g (1 lb 2 oz) green beans, trimmed
    and cut in half widthways
2 tomatoes, peeled, cored and chopped
15 g (¼ cup) roughly chopped mint
1 tbsp sugar
200 g (7 oz) samphire
Lemon wedges, to serve
Sea salt and freshly ground black pepper

METHOD

Preheat the oven to 180°C (350°F). Sauté the onion and garlic in the olive oil until soft.

Mix together all the other ingredients except the samphire and place in a baking dish. Season with ½ teaspoon salt and pepper. Cover with foil and bake in the oven until very soft, around 20 minutes. When it's almost done, add the samphire.

Season to taste and serve with the lemon wedges.

HERB SALAD AND GINGER-LIME DRESSING

SERVES 4

This salad is best eaten the day it is made or let it steep overnight and have it with crusty bread and smoked fish.

INGREDIENTS

4 generous handfuls of mixed herbs, such as
  parsley, coriander (cilantro), opal basil,
  Thai basil, lemon basil, chives, tarragon,
  mint, shiso, dill and fennel fronds
85 g (¾ cup) cherry tomatoes, halved
1 cucumber, cut into rounds

GINGER·LIME DRESSING

1 tbsp lime juice
1 medium–hot green or red chilli, preferably
  Fresno, minced
1 red Asian shallot, minced
4 cm (1½ inch) piece of fresh ginger, peeled
1 garlic clove
½ tsp honey
125 ml (½ cup) extra virgin olive oil
Sea salt and freshly ground black pepper

METHOD

To make the ginger-lime dressing, in a small bowl, combine the lime juice, chilli and shallot. Using a fine grater or Microplane, grate the ginger and garlic into the bowl. Add the honey and gradually whisk in the olive oil until well combined. Season with salt and pepper.

In a salad bowl, combine the mixed herbs, cherry tomatoes and cucumber. Season with salt and pepper. Drizzle in up to 60 ml (¼ cup) of the dressing and gently toss. The dressing should coat the herbs, but not weigh them down. Any spare dressing can be stored in an airtight container in the refrigerator for up to 3 days.

CHOPPED SALAD

SERVES 4

This salad is a little dirty, I admit. But it's delicious and one of those salads that is the first to get eaten at a family barbecue. Never apologise for being dirty because it's what most people want, anyway.

OREGANO VINAIGRETTE

2½ tbsp red wine vinegar
2 tbsp oregano leaves
Juice of ½ lemon, plus more to taste
2 garlic cloves, 1 smashed and 1 grated
200 ml (generous ¾ cup) extra virgin olive oil
Sea salt and freshly ground black pepper

SALAD

½ small red onion, halved through the core
1 small head of iceberg lettuce
1 radicchio
500 g (1 lb 2 oz) bloody good tomatoes, quartered
500 g (1 lb 2 oz) aged provolone, sliced
  3 mm (⅛ inch) thick and cut into
  5–6 mm (¼ inch) strips
250 g (9 oz) Genoa salami, sliced 3 mm (⅛ inch)
  thick and cut into 5–6 mm (¼ inch) strips
5 pepperoncini, stems discarded, thinly sliced

METHOD

To make the dressing, whisk together the vinegar, oregano, lemon juice, garlic, salt and pepper in a medium bowl. Let the mixture rest for 5 minutes to marinate the oregano. Add the oil in a slow, steady stream, whisking constantly to form an emulsified vinaigrette. Taste for seasoning, and add more salt or lemon juice as needed. Any leftover dressing can be refrigerated for another use for up to 3 days.

To make the salad, separate the layers of the onion and stack two or three layers on top of one another, then cut them lengthways into 2 mm (1/16 inch) wide strips. Repeat with the remaining onion layers. Place the onion in a small bowl of iced water to sit while you prepare the rest of the ingredients.

Cut the iceberg lettuce in half through the core. Remove and discard the outer leaves and cut out and discard the core. Separate the lettuce leaves and stack two or three leaves on top of one another, then cut them lengthways into 5–6 mm (¼ inch) wide strips. Repeat with the remaining leaves, slicing the radicchio in the same way.

Season the tomatoes with salt to taste, and toss gently. Drain the onion and pat dry with paper towel before adding to a large, wide bowl.

Combine the lettuce, radicchio, tomatoes, provolone, salami, pepperoncini and onion in the bowl. Season with salt to taste and toss to make sure the leaves are coated.

Drizzle 6 tablespoons of the oregano vinaigrette over the salad, tossing gently to coat the salad evenly. Taste, then add the remaining 2 tablespoons of the vinaigrette, plus salt or lemon juice as needed.

Transfer the salad to a large platter or divide it among individual plates, piling it up like an obscene mountain.

138

BEETROOT SALAD OF THE GODS

SERVES 2

Another easy beetroot salad, this one was inspired by my favourite London restaurant, the quintessentially English St. John. One of the very few restaurants in the world I pine for; their respect for food and wine is inspiring without being overly sentimental. It makes me cry and go hard at the same time. Kind of like the bedroom scene in *The Crying Game*.

INGREDIENTS

200 ml (generous ¾ cup) extra virgin olive oil
100 ml (scant ½ cup) aged balsamic vinegar
150 g (generous ½ cup) crème fraîche
1 tbsp capers
2 raw beetroot, peeled and finely grated
¼ red cabbage, core cut out, very finely sliced
1 small red onion, finely sliced
2 bunches of chervil, leaves picked
Sea salt and freshly ground white pepper

METHOD

Throw everything into the bowl, keeping back a few chervil leaves, and mix thoroughly with your hands. Season very well and garnish with the leaves.

Then go online and order heaps of the St. John Claret. Send me some while you are at it.

SHEBA

SERVES 4

The only real accompaniment for Pap. Variations of this sauce are found all over Africa, but this version was the one I learnt at age 3 from my second mother, Julia Ledwaba. This spicy tomato gravy is one of the foundations of Southern African cooking and any Saffa who says otherwise is full of shit.

INGREDIENTS

2 onions, finely chopped
2 tbsp olive oil
2 or more garlic cloves, crushed
4 large ripe tomatoes, finely chopped,
  or 400 g (14 oz) tin plum tomatoes,
  chopped (don't drain)
1 roasted and skinned green capsicum (pepper)
¼ tsp sugar
1 tsp curry powder
2 hot chillies, diced
Sea salt and freshly ground black pepper

METHOD

Lightly brown the onion in the oil in a saucepan. Add the remaining ingredients and cook briskly, uncovered, for about 10 minutes until the sauce has thickened.

PAP

SERVES 4

Pap is the African carb staple, which is eaten with every single meal, every single day. I love the stuff – it's the perfect vehicle to transport flavour into your gob. It's basically a finely milled polenta and cooks the same way. Enjoy with Sheba and grilled meats.

INGREDIENTS

3 litres (12 cups) chicken stock
250 g (1 cup) butter
450 g (1 lb) maize meal
Sea salt

METHOD

In a large saucepan, bring the stock to the boil over high heat. Add the butter and allow it to melt. Gradually rain in all of the ground maize, stirring constantly as it cooks and thickens.

Start by boiling it, stirring as you go, then lower the heat to medium to thicken it, then turn to a low heat for a few minutes.

After approximately 5–10 minutes, it will start to come away from the sides of the pan. This is a sign it's ready.

Cover, remove from the heat and allow to steam for 15 minutes. Season with salt before serving.

FIG I. SHEBA

SHALLOT PANCAKES

MAKES 6 PANCAKES

Please make this recipe before you get high. I love eating these as dippers for my mapo tofu (page 127). They're so good they are pretty much pornographic.

INGREDIENTS

600 g (4 cups) plain flour
65 g (2 oz) vegetable shortening
2 tsp sea salt, plus extra to sprinkle
100 ml (3½ fl oz) sesame oil
6 tbsp minced spring onions (scallions)
Vegetable oil, for frying

METHOD

Combine 150 g (1 cup) of the flour with the shortening in a stand mixer fitted with a dough hook. Mix on low speed until the fat is dispersed into tiny clumps. Pour 150 ml (generous ½ cup) warm water into the bowl and mix for about 3 minutes until a stiff dough forms. Stop the mixer and then add the remaining flour, salt and 2½ tablespoons water. Knead on medium speed for 3 minutes. The dough will be smooth and supple and hold a fingerprint indefinitely. Wrap the dough in plastic wrap and let rest for 10 minutes or refrigerate for up to 2 days.

Unwrap the dough and cut it into six equal pieces. Roll the pieces into balls and drape with plastic wrap so they don't dry out as you work. Lightly flour your work surface and use a rolling pin to roll one of the balls out into a 20–23 cm (8–9 inch) round. Brush the entire surface of the dough generously with sesame oil and sprinkle with 1 tablespoon spring onions.

Sprinkle lightly with salt. Now roll the dough into a log of greenish pancake dough. Form the log into a tight spiral, creating a tight roll. Repeat with the remaining dough, sesame oil, spring onions and salt until you have made six rolls. Let them rest for at least 10 minutes. (They can also be individually wrapped in plastic wrap and refrigerated for up to 1 day at this point.)

Now it is time to flatten the rolls. Lightly flour your work surface. Have two or three goes with the rolling pin, gently flattening each disc as you go, then turn it 90 degrees and repeat. Keep going until it's about 20 cm (8 inches) in diameter.

Square the dough by cutting off the edges to make a 7 cm (3 inch) square.

Place 1 teaspoon of filling in the middle of each square of dough. Dip your finger in a bowl of water and run it along two edges of the square. Fold the square into a triangle, pressing the top together and then working your way along the sides. Draw the bottom two corners of the triangle together to form a kerchief shape. Press tightly to seal. Toss with a little flour, set aside on a well-floured baking sheet, and cover.

Heat 3 mm (⅛ inch) vegetable oil in a large pan over medium heat. Fry the pancakes for 5–6 minutes total, flipping once, until very crisp and browned. Cut into wedges and serve hot.

ANCHOVY-BRAISED GREENS

SERVES 4

It's safe to say this is one of my favourite ways to eat greens. The umami flavours from the anchovy are slightly diluted by the water in the vegetables, which makes a great little sauce for something meatier.

INGREDIENTS

1 long red chilli, bruised
2 bunches of kale, trimmed and
   cut into 4 cm (1½ inch) lengths
Large pinch of white sugar
1 tbsp Bagna cauda (page 201)
Dash of fish sauce

METHOD

Heat a frying pan until very hot. Add the chilli and char for 4–6 minutes until blackened.

Add the kale and stir-fry vigorously for about 20–30 seconds until wilted. Add 1 tablespoon water and the sugar and simmer for a moment, stirring to combine. Add the bagna cauda, season with fish sauce and serve.

SIGARA BOREGI

SERVES 4

This dish is very kitsch, but it's also freaking delicious. Make heaps as they freeze really well.

INGREDIENTS

200 g (7 oz) firm feta cheese
¼ bunch of dill, leaves chopped
¼ bunch of flat-leaf parsley, chopped
½ a pack of filo sheets
100 g (⅓ cup) melted butter
500 ml (2 cups) vegetable oil
Freshly ground black pepper
Mint sauce or fermented hot sauce, to serve

METHOD

Grate the feta into a bowl and mix with the herbs and pepper.

Lay the filo sheets on your worktop and lightly brush the sheets with a little of the butter.

Take the feta mix, evenly spread over the sheets and roll into cigar shapes. Chill in the fridge for 30 minutes, then slice into 1 cm (½ inch) thick slices.

Heat the oil in a deep saucepan. When hot, drop in the discs and fry for about 3 minutes each side until golden.

Drain well and serve with mint sauce or fermented hot sauce or both – why not?

BUFFALO FETA AND PISTACHIO SALAD

SERVES 4

Only use the finest feta for this salad! Don't skimp, the apocalypse is nigh and no-one wants to eat polystyrene just yet.

BRIOCHE CROUTONS

1 brioche loaf
Knob of butter
250 g (9 oz) buffalo feta or any other
  soft feta in olive oil

HERB SALAD

2 bunches of tarragon, leaves picked
1 bunch of flat-leaf parsley, leaves picked
1 bunch of dill, sprigs picked
1 bunch of chervil, sprigs picked
¼ bunch of chives, cut into 2 cm (¾ inch) lengths
Drizzle of olive oil

SAGE AND PISTACHIO DRESSING

100 ml (scant ½ cup) extra virgin olive oil
4 garlic cloves, thinly sliced
½ bunch of sage, leaves picked
100 ml (scant ½ cup) balsamic vinegar
Juice of ½ lemon
140 g (1 cup) shelled unsalted pistachio
  nuts, toasted
1 tsp rosewater
Sea salt and freshly ground black pepper

METHOD

To make the croutons, cut the brioche loaf into six 2.5 cm (1 inch) slices and, using a 6 cm (2½ inch) ring cutter, cut out six discs.

Gently fry the brioche discs in butter until they are lightly browned on both sides.

Mould the feta cheese into six discs of the same diameter as the croutons. Place on top of the croutons and set aside.

To make the salad, mix together all the herbs, cover and place in the fridge until needed.

To make the sage and pistachio dressing, heat the olive oil and fry the garlic until golden. Strain and reserve the garlic. Heat the oil again and fry the sage leaves until crisp. Strain and reserve the leaves. Remove the oil from the heat.

Add the balsamic vinegar, lemon juice, pistachio nuts, rosewater and the cooked sage leaves and garlic to the oil. Season with salt and pepper.

To assemble, place the feta cheese croutons into a hot oven and allow the cheese to warm through for 5 minutes or until melted.

Dress the herb salad with a little olive oil, salt and pepper. Place in the middle of six plates and form a hole in the middle of each salad big enough to just fit a crouton, then add the warm croutons.

Gently warm the sage and pistachio dressing, stir well and ladle a little over each crouton.

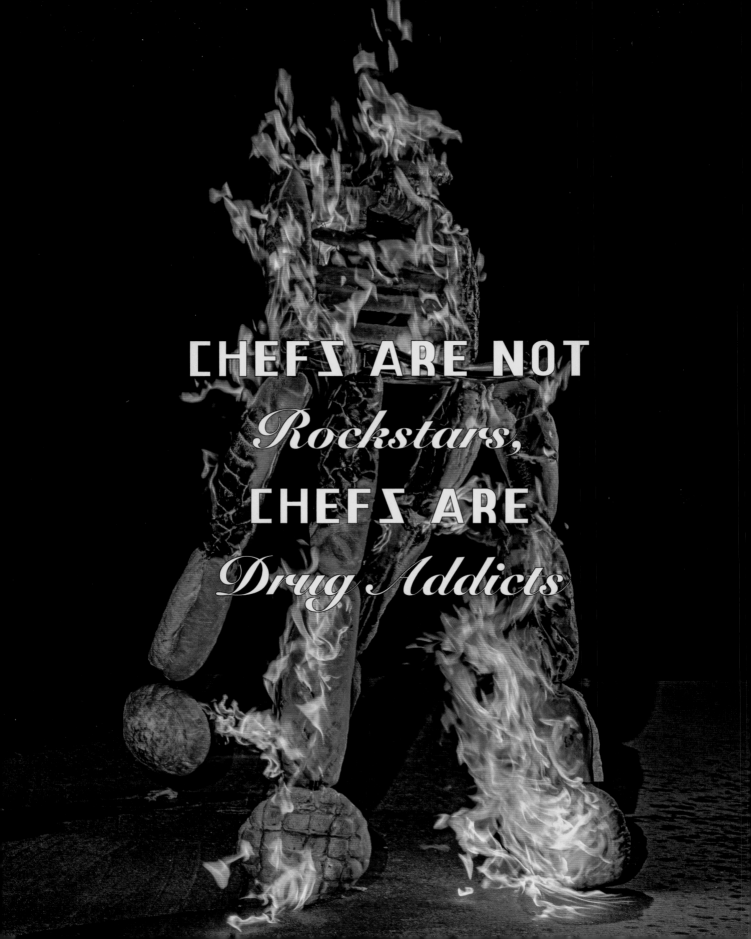

During the past few decades, celebrity culture's grip on our society has tightened. Yes, celebrities have been part of the cultural landscape for most of human history and whether it's Alexander the Great or Michael Jackson, people have always been fascinated with the famous, but never before has celebrity chef culture played such a prominent role in so many aspects of our everyday lives. It has a measurable influence on individual decisions – the things we do to stay healthy, how we view ourselves physically, the material goods we want to possess, the restaurants we eat at and our future career aspirations.

Whether we like it or not, celebrity chef culture has had an impact on the world, framing how we think about important issues and even influencing how we view our place on this planet and within our industry. Celebrity culture is often blamed for dumbing down our social discourse, but less has been said about how celebrity chef culture has influenced us for good, but more importantly for bad.

Indeed, celebrity chefs have emerged as one of the most significant and influential sources of information when it comes to the way people eat, cook and shop, and even how to bollock incompetent staff. On one hand they champion huge supermarket brands, turning a blind eye to how the products are actually being produced, while on the other they speak about supporting local farmers and being concerned for our environment. Their social views seem to shift and evolve for no other reason than to promote their brands.

BUT WE ARE ALL HYPOCRITES

The hypocrisy fills our cultural landscape with notions that range from those that are absurd and widely mocked, such as Gwyneth Paltrow's *Eat Pray Love* fundamentalist propaganda website, *Goop*, or Guy Fieri's range of completely useless kitchen equipment – 'These tools of the trade are designed to my exact specifications and are used at home and in my restaurants.' Fuck off, Guy. No self-respecting chef would tip up to work sporting your knives, not unless they were an extra in a new food-based romantic comedy starring Catherine Zeta Jones and you're the pleb making a fucking poke bowl in the background – to Tom Kerridge's dangerous comments about how women just don't have the fire in their bellies to become top chefs. We shouldn't even be discussing this shit today, but here we are. (Side note: the most thoughtful, methodical, passionate chefs I know are women.) Equally, Gordon Ramsay being aghast at the level of drug use found in his kitchens, even though everyone knows hospitality pretty much contributes 95 per cent of the annual Colombian GDP. And by the way, *Gordon Ramsay on Cocaine* wasn't actually a show about Ramsay doing heaps of rack, but explored how deep substance abuse is embedded in the UK and especially in hospitality. Besides, can you imagine Gordon actually on coke, fuck me! Even more shouty, abusive, always on edge, constantly talking about himself and his restaurants. What a kitchen nightmare!

Of course, there are some projects that gain substantial social traction and market appeal for good, such as René Redzepi's MAD symposiums, Massimo Bottura's socially conscious project Food for Soul, Norbert Niederkofler's thoughtful mountain movement CARE's and Ronni Kahn's mission to feed the homeless in Australia with her incredible charity OzHarvest. On the other end of the spectrum, these promote diversity, social and environmental responsibility.

However, sadly issues such as sustainability, foraging, fermentation, the preservation of indigenous cultures and the championing of new agricultural practices obviously get less of a platform than the fuck-ton of reality television shows, with their fresh-faced and cult-eyed 'cooks', professional or otherwise, reappearing every few days in front of us, spewing endlessly onto our televisions like consignments of baby chickens being tossed through the doors of a Macca's chicken-nugget factory.

The whole thing resembles an Orwellian novel in which terrified citizens have to watch and engage with this farce to stay culturally relevant around the water cooler, otherwise they will be executed in front of their co-workers. So basically, Amazon.

AND THESE SHOWS ARE EVERYWHERE

Celebrities have the capacity to cast a spell on us all. Shows like *Masterchef, Iron Chef, Chef's Table* and *The Final Table* leverage this fascination. The promise of becoming a celebrity is the unspoken reward for appearing on the show.

Celebrity culture is more than just a real interest in celebrities. It is a true reflection of our collective values and a manifestation of the complex interplay between social expectations and harsher socioeconomic realities. As the sociologist Karen Sternheimer writes in *Celebrity Culture and the American Dream*, 'Rather than simple superficial distractions, celebrity and fame are unique manifestations of our sense of social mobility: They provide the illusion that material wealth is possible for anyone ... Celebrities seem to provide proof that the American Dream of rising from rags to riches is real and attainable.'

Which is a bloody attractive proposition if you're in hospitality earning minimum wage. Indeed, it is often sold as magic: a life-changing process that is now – or so the celebrity myth goes – increasingly available to all, particularly chefs.

For corporations to sell their messages to the detriment of our communities, it helps them for us chefs to provide endorsement first because no-one really questions celebrity chefs. There is no Royal Commission or any government or public oversight on ethics. Our natural habitat is the kitchen, not congress.

THIS IS VERY DANGEROUS

An example of this was Jamie Oliver's Garden campaign, where he became the face of Woolworths Australia, promoting fresh fruit and vegetables with his stamp of approval. Jamie received millions of dollars for this particular campaign and Middle Australia lapped it up, furthering Jamie Oliver's reputation of giving a shit about what people eat while championing farmers.

The flip side of all this was that vegetable farmers were being charged 40¢ a crate to fund the Jamie's Garden advertising campaign on top of an existing marketing levy. One large supplier paid $300,000 over the six-week campaign, according to the industry's peak supply group AUSVEG. Imagine the extra pressure that was placed on smaller operators working on 'wafer-thin' profit margins.

DID JAMIE NEED THOSE MILLIONS OF DOLLARS?

I'm pretty sure those farmers could have done without that particular marketing campaign. A dubious marketing strategy by big business, with one of the most trusted faces on TV, paid for by hard-working Australians working in one of the most unforgiving industries. A disgraceful initiative and counterproductive to promoting the 'eat local' tagline, especially when many farmers have disappeared through bankruptcy or worse.

On a more fundamental level, chef celebrity culture has contributed to the rise of a more narcissistic and selfish industry. I remember first starting out as a commis chef and being told: 'Cooking is only a third of the job ... the rest is cleaning.'

TO ME, THAT MADE SENSE

Nowadays, cooking is only a fifth of the job, the rest is PR management, social media algorithms, trolling Mario Batali on Twitter and deleting my internet browser history.

We have become obsessed about staying relevant in a world where there are fewer staff, but more young entrepreneurs. The pie is getting smaller and smaller every day and our business models keep shifting and evolving to accommodate market trends to the detriment of our existing staff, our own families and business partners. (BTW this angst isn't because HBO didn't pick up my new reality cooking show, *Silly Hair and Shit Cooks*.)

This is a determining factor as to why we still cling on to a media that constantly exploits us because, God forbid, they stop writing about us, stop asking us to appear on their shows or, even worse, we drop places on their imaginary lists. Instead they pay us a meagre sum of money (or none at all) to promote their products, their events, their lists, their bullshit, so their sponsors can circle jerk over our mental health and values while reviewing their end-of-year financials. We have become complicit in this out of fear of going broke or losing face.

I SAY FUCK THEM!

My hospitality brothers and sisters, don't ever forget that these organisations need you! Without you, they have no content and no friendly and familiar professional faces selling their products. It's time for us to take back that power and focus on the issues that are important to us: our communities, our growers, our artisans and our families.

We cannot lose sight of the reason we started in this industry in the first place. Not to be famous, not because we were pretty much unemployable in any other industry … it's because we actually wanted to service our communities and bring joy to people. Like Patch Adams, only with less dying. We are drug addicts, and our drug is watching the faces of our customers enjoying our food, bringing joy into people's lives and our own through cooking and eating and drinking.

It's safe to say we may never become super famous and make hundreds of millions of dollars in media like Jamie Oliver or Heston Blumenthal or Gordon Ramsay. However, we cannot be complicit in the destruction of our communities and industry because we bought into what these chefs were selling.

Battle lines have been drawn, the old guard has let us down and our planet and society cannot afford it anymore. So chefs, when that email hits your inbox to endorse a product, to appear on that show or to attend an event, think not only about what you stand for; it's time for us to think about what THEY stand for as well.

04

ACID
trip

WE LOVE FUNK IN OUR FOOD AT AFRICOLA.
BECAUSE OUR FOOD CAN BE DESCRIBED AS RICH AND FULL OF
FLAVOUR, YOU NEED THAT ACID TO CUT RIGHT THROUGH IT AND
CLEANSE THE TONGUE FOR THE NEXT MOUTHFUL. I'VE INCLUDED HERE
SOME WEIRDO RECIPES FROM MY HOMELAND, A KOJI MASTERCLASS
BY THE BEST FERMENTER I KNOW (ADAM JAMES, ROUGH RICE) AND
BUCKET WINE BY ONE OF MY FAVOURITE WINEMAKERS IN THE WORLD,
THE OCHOTA FAMILY. SO PLEASE MAKE A CUPPA, PUT YOUR FEET
UP AND 'TURN ON, TUNE IN, DROP OUT'.

INTRODUCTION
BY
Adam James
ROUGH RICE

My first venture into the world of fermentation was at age 14 in boarding school. I combined aniseed essence, sugar and warm water in 2-litre coke bottles and stashed them under my bed. Lo and behold, several weeks later, I ended up with a face-cringingly potent, long-lost relative of sambuca. It was vile yet legitimate tender in boarding school and was used to influence and barter for all manner of things (both legal and otherwise). Of course, I eventually got caught, intoxicated on my own brew, and would have been expelled had I technically not done anything illegal – all ingredients were acquired from the supermarket and how was I to know what would happen by mixing them together?

Much later in life, while running Tricycle Café in Hobart, I became legitimately fascinated by the alchemy of fermentation: how with a little salt and time you can literally transform an ingredient into something completely amazing. I was mainly dabbling in quite simple lacto-ferments – pickles, hot sauces, sauerkrauts and kimchis – yet as a cook, the flavour profiles created were so, so delicious.

From there, hobby became obsession and Rough Rice was born in 2014. I started investing any spare money I had into large ceramic crocks and set up my own fermentary. I would read anything I could get my hands on and all of my spare time was put into research and experimentation. I also travelled as much as I could (mainly around Asia – including an annual pilgrimage to Japan) to expand my knowledge. I started delving more into the world of cultured ferments, making koji, misos, doubanjiang, gochujang and so forth.

In 2017 I was fortunate to land a Churchill Fellowship and went on a 'fermentation world tour' that took me to Denmark, Italy, France, Georgia, China, Korea and Japan to study age-old (and new) fermentation techniques. Whilst I was away, the café sold and now fermentation (and making fermented condiments) is my primary focus. I'm now getting more experimental, playing with traditional techniques and methodology and adapting them to local ingredients. Like a good wine, every vintage is unique, and no two condiments will ever be the same – a real pain in the arse for marketing purposes.

I currently supply a select handful of restaurants around the country and am proud to say that Duncan and Africola placed my very first legitimate order. I still supply them and absolutely love how they implement my creations into their menu.

AMAZI

★ ★ ★

Amazi is considered a delicacy in the Zulu culture. As a teenager, we used to drink it to try and get a buzz, but drinking sour curdled milk to get drunk is as effective as smoking nutmeg to get high. This is an acquired taste, but I would recommend to the adventurous. Amazi is largely milk, allowed to curdle in a gourd or basket, the whey being removed through a hole in the base and drunk. Once finished, it is refilled with fresh milk. The curds act as a 'mother', if you will, and that bacteria keeps evolving, developing a deeper flavour with every new milk added.

UMꚈOMBOTHI

★ ★ ★

Beer is central to the social culture of the Zulu people. I remember going on a school trip from Johannesburg to Shakaland, which is basically the set from the famous drama series about *Shaka Zulu* turned into a traditional learning centre and tourist attraction. It was there among the topless tribes women (I was just 8 years old) that we were shown how to make and drink Umqombothi.

Umqombothi is made from a native sorghum (*Sorghum bicolor*) and is only brewed by the badass women in the tribe. It is made in a hut that is not completely thatched, so the temperature from the fire can incubate the yeast and smoke can escape so that the beer gets enough oxygen to allow it to ferment. Very clever indeed! It is an excellent thirst quencher, particularly in the hot African sun, and it is also very nutritious and known to soothe stomach ulcers.

The general method involves cooking maize and sorghum to form a thick porridge, which is then left to stand for one day to cool and steep and get all funky. On the second day, the softened grains are boiled with water to form a milky soup and dried sorghum is sprinkled on top, as you would sprinkle koji over a ferment. The large pot is covered to keep it warm and aid the fermentation process (it also keeps the flies and dust out) for one day. Once fermented, the beer is passed through a grass sieve and served.

There is a specific way that Zulu beer is traditionally served. The ritual is started by the woman who brewed the beer. She skims the froth off and pours it on the ground next to a ukhamba (clay pot) as an offering (*kwabaphansi*) to her ancestors, who always drink first, kind of like 'this one's for my homies'. The beer is then stirred and a hollowed-out gourd is filled. The kneeling hostess drinks first in front of all the guests to prove that the beer is safe to drink. The host then drinks to check the quality and if he is satisfied, his guests are served, in order of status.

One must always drink sitting or squatting and the men must take off their hats as a sign of respect to the hosts. Everyone takes a long swig as it can take a while for the beer to be passed around. If the gourd is placed mouth up, it indicates that you want a refill; if it is placed mouth down on its base, it means you have had enough. The beer does get you progressively drunk, which I find super cool because of the small amount of time the fermentation needs to produce the alcohol, which can sometimes be as much a 3%.

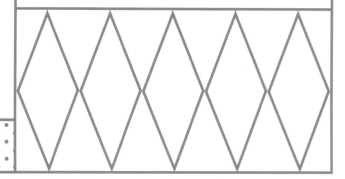

FIG 1. AMAZI (X2). KOJI GRAINS AND BARLEY. KANZURI

KOJI

MAKES 2 JARS

Koji (*Aspergillus oryzae*) is not a yeast as many people mistakenly believe. It is actually a filamentous fungus, originally found in rice stalks, and is integral to the making of fermented foods (and alcoholic drinks) around Asia. Its history dates back to China some nine thousand years ago. In Japan it is called koji and is used to make sake, miso, shoyu (soy sauce), mirin and rice vinegars (amongst other things).

Last year I spent several days making koji and miso in an incredible sixth-generation koji house in Shimizu. There were never any measurements, timers or thermometers (my kind of fermentation), but it's best to follow the 'rules' the first couple of times.

The process for making koji may be time consuming, but it is in fact quite simple and very rewarding. Koji-kin is available online.

INGREDIENTS

500 g (2½ cups) short-grain sushi rice
  (preferably premium Koshihikari rice)
10 g (¼ oz) powdered koji-kin

EQUIPMENT

Steamer
Cooking thermometer
Sterilised bowl
Large tray and muslin cloth
Egg incubator (optional)

METHOD

Soak the rice overnight, then steam in a steamer at 100°C (212°F) for about 1½ hours until tender. Remove from the steamer and allow to cool to 35°C (95°F) degrees, testing the temperature with a cooking thermometer.

Place the rice into a sterilised bowl and sprinkle with powdered koji-kin. Carefully mix until well combined with the rice.

Arrange a muslin cloth on a tray large enough for the rice to be spread roughly 1 cm (½ in) deep. Spread the rice carefully and evenly.

Cover with a clean damp cloth that has been sterilised in boiling water and allowed to cool.

Using an egg incubator or your oven turned on to pilot, set a temperature of 30°C (86°F). Place the rice in the incubator and leave for 18 hours. It is crucial that the temperature doesn't rise above 35°C (95°F) as this may kill the spores.

Remove the tray and aerate the rice to distribute spores. This can be done with clean fingers in a raking motion. The rice should smell fragrant and, well, delicious. Check the temperature – again you're aiming for somewhere between 30–35°C (86–95°F).

Return the rice to the incubator and repeat the process every 6 hours for a further 18 hours. At this point the rice should bind together. Separate the grains using your clean hands.

Koji can be used immediately or preserved in a salt brine (shio koji) and spread out in a large tray to dry. It will keep in the fridge for a couple of weeks and can also be frozen for later use.

KANZURI

MAKES 2 JARS

I first tried this delectable condiment in a tiny sake bar in Kyoto. The tiniest dollop was served on a cube of fresh tofu and it blew me away. It was equal parts salty, spicy, citrusy and umami. When I learnt of the process I was even more fascinated. Made in the Niigata prefecture, togarashi chillies are buried in snow then mixed with koji, yuzu peel and salt. Amazing. I have since dedicated my life to trying to replicate it.

This bastardised version doesn't involve burying chillies in snow, or yuzu (as they're very hard to come across in Tasmania), but instead uses preserved lemons and I add shiso, Vietnamese mint and pepperberry for extra fragrance. It's not a legitimate kanzuri, but it does taste pretty fucking good.

INGREDIENTS

200 g (7 oz) preserved lemons, skin only
   (flesh and seeds removed)
100 g (3½ oz) Koji (see opposite)
250 g (9 oz) medium-heat chillies (I use
   rocotos with stems and seeds removed)
450 g (1 lb) turnip or daikon
½ bunch of purple shiso, leaves picked
½ bunch of Vietnamese mint,
   leaves picked
Big pinch of ground pepperberry
   (or sancho pepper)
Non-iodised sea salt

EQUIPMENT

Sterilised ceramic crock or a couple of
   glass jars with an airlock

METHOD

Combine all the ingredients in a food processor and blend until smooth. The consistency should be thick but pourable. Add filtered water, if necessary, to loosen.

Taste – it should be sufficiently salty from the preserved lemons, but add more to taste. It should be salty.

Transfer to a ceramic crock or a couple of glass jars. Sprinkle the surface lightly with salt to help prevent any undesirables. If you're using a jar with a screw lid, you'll have to burp it periodically as CO_2 builds. Ideally the kanzuri paste will nearly fill the vessel, minimising exposure to oxygen.

Leave at room temperature for at least a month before transferring to the fridge. If a white film appears on the surface fret not, this is kahm yeast and is perfectly safe; just scrape it off. If other colours appear, then best to discard and try again.

After a month it is ready to go, but does improve with age. My current batch is 18 months old and the flavours have really concentrated and intensified.

Eat me with anything – it's particularly good with raw fish and octopus.

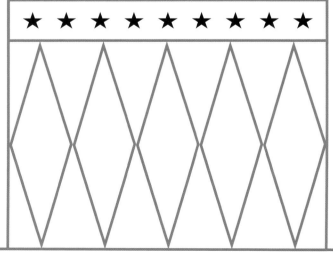

GARLIC DILL PICKLES

MAKES 6 JARS

I have never not had a jar of these in my larder. When the pickles are finished, make sure you save the brine for picklebacks or try to pass it off to co-workers as kombucha. Don't be dogmatic when following this recipe. Add what you feel, go wild. Chilli flakes, whole chillies, who cares?

INGREDIENTS

2 kg (4 lb 8 oz) Lebanese cucumbers
1 litre (4 cups) apple cider vinegar
1 litre (4 cups) filtered water
4 tbsp pickling salt
12 garlic cloves, peeled
2 tbsp dill seed
2 tsp celery seeds
4 tsp black peppercorns
2 tsp red chilli flakes

EQUIPMENT

6 x 500 ml (17 fl oz) jars

METHOD

Wash the jars thoroughly in warm, soapy water. Place in boiling water to sterilise the jars and then dry in a hot oven for a few minutes.

Wash and dry the cucumbers. Remove the blossom ends. Cut into chips, spears or leave whole, depending on your preference.

Combine the vinegar, water and salt in a saucepan and bring to the boil.

Equally divide the garlic cloves, dill and celery seeds, black peppercorns and chilli flakes among the jars.

Pack the prepared cucumbers into the jars as tightly as you can without crushing them and then pour the brine into the jars, leaving 5–6 mm (¼ in) headspace (that's the amount of space between the surface of the brine and the rim of the jar).

These pickles will keep for at least 6 months in the fridge or at room temperature, but probably won't last for more than a week because they are that delicious.

BOOM CHAKKALAKA

SERVES 4

Chakkalaka is a traditional condiment served on the tables of most South African households. It's usually made up of root vegetables, curry powder, vegetable oil and baked beans. The best version is found in a tin and I'll argue with anyone that says they could make better. This is our slightly weirdo version. The kombucha vinegar will help it go a little funky and gives depth of flavour, which will make the radicchio taste a little meatier and slightly cabbagey – in a good way.

INGREDIENTS

100 ml (scant ½ cup) rapeseed oil
2 bulbs of garlic, cloves peeled
    and finely chopped
10 curry leaves
1 hot chilli, cut in half
1 tsp madras curry powder
Zest of 2 lemons
100 ml (scant ½ cup) kombucha vinegar
5 radicchios, trimmed and quartered

EQUIPMENT

Cooking thermometer
Barbecue or skillet

METHOD

Put all the ingredients apart from the vinegar and radicchio in a saucepan and bring up to 70°C (158°F). Let the mixture infuse off the heat until cool, then add the vinegar.

Meanwhile, slightly char the radicchio on a hot skillet or barbecue if it's on, until the leaves start to fray. Pour all the liquids over it and leave to marinate overnight or longer for a more intense flavour.

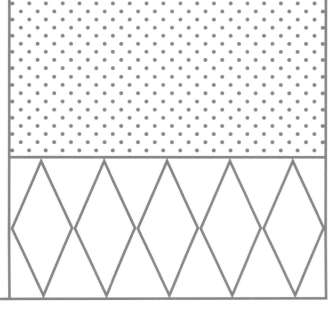

THE OCHOTA

Fresh Wine

DISCO ™

TARAƧ, AMBER, + ANOUK
[ƧAGE ABƧENT: BUƧY DRAWING ƧWORDƧ]

Taras and Amber Ochota have steadily been changing the wine landscape in Australia with their wine label Ochota Barrels, fuelled by their love of the Adelaide Hills and hardcore music. Taras Ochota used to play bass in hardcore band Kranktus and most of their wines take their names from punk songs by The Stranglers, The Pixies and Dead Kennedys, or phrases found on the backs of amplifiers. They even made a collaborative wine called 'Sense of Compression' with music legend Maynard James Keenan from one of my favourite bands – Tool. 'Our approach to wine is very hands on,' says Taras, 'and we don't do much to the grapes – we just try to coerce them into an elegant, feminine style. We pick the fruit earlier, so our wines have an almost edgy, nervous tension, I suppose – similar to the music we like. We're not into high alcohol and lashings of oak. We're into wines with energy and vibrancy.'

Over this page are two recipes: the first one is what they call 'Bucket Wine', basically a super fresh boozy wine anyone can attempt at home. The second is a recipe from Taras's mum, Lili, and is an epic Ukranian dumpling to line the stomach while smashing this disco juice.

PUSSY SAUSAGE BUCKET WINE BY TARAS OCHOTA

EQUIPMENT

2 x 20 litre (40 pint) plastic
  food-grade buckets
1 pair of snippers
Cover cloth for buckets
Elastic band to fit around the top
  of each bucket
1 large colander
1 large sieve
A pretty 5 litre (11 pint) minimum vessel
  to ladle wine from, with pretty tea cups

WARNING

Who knows what the alcohol level is, so eat
with a few of Duncan's gorgeous recipes next
to a sofa with lots of close friends.

METHOD

Preferably find a good organic pinot noir or
grenache grower, but anything is fine really.
Give him/her a carton of non-hoppy beer.
(Yuck! Who wants to drink bong water.)
Something that is thirst quenching, crisp
and clean.

Ask if they can let you know before the grapes
are all picked and if you can grab a bucket.

If super keen, taste the grapes on the vines
every few days or so when they are close to
ripeness, until you just can't stop eating
them. This is the day you pick. Drink a few
shots of mezcal to sanitise yourself, then fill
bucket one with whole bunches.

Zoom back home, get naked if not already,
and squash the grapes into that same bucket
with your fist or face or whatever, so it is now
half full of berries and juice.

You are now a winemaker.

Cover the top of the bucket with the cloth
and fit the elastic band so vinegar flies,
Toggenburg goats or curious children can't
get in. Place in a warm spot, about 25°C
(77°F).

Once a day, submerge the cover cloth into
the juice with your clean hands and taste the
juice. One day (7–14 days in … maybe
longer) you will taste it where you can't
stop tasting it. This day, drain the juice into
bucket two through the colander. Once the
juice is all drained, fill the colander with
berries and stalks.

Press the juice out with your clean hands
in small batches until bucket one is empty.
Give the pressed stalks and berries to the
Toggenburg goat.

Clean bucket one with water and a new
sponge, then sieve bucket two into bucket
one. Repeat this step.

Cover again and in a few days, or when it
tastes like natural wine, drink naked with
friends from a pretty vessel with pretty
tea cups.

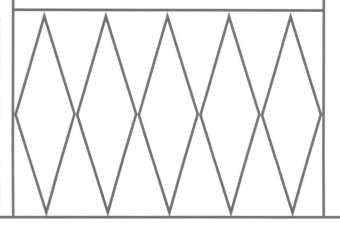

TARAS'S MUM'S VARENYKY (PYROHY) UKRAINIAN DUMPLINGS RECIPE

MAKES 20 DUMPLINGS

This is delicious cement for the stomach. Eat too many of these and you will stop altogether. Edible rigor mortis.

SOFT DOUGH

300 g (2 cups) plain flour, sifted
1 tsp sea salt
1 egg yolk, beaten
1 tbsp sunflower oil
125 ml (½ cup) warm water

POTATO AND CHEESE FILLING

2 tbsp grated onion
2 tbsp butter
460 g (2 cups) hot mashed potato
100 g (1 cup) grated cheddar cheese, or more
Sea salt and freshly ground white pepper

BEURRE NOISETTE

150 g (⅔ cup) melted butter

TO SERVE

150 ml (generous ½ cup) sour cream
100 g (3½ oz) crispy bacon bits

METHOD

To make the soft dough, knead the ingredients together lightly in a bowl for 3 minutes, adding a little more water as required, then divide in two. Wrap in plastic wrap to rest for 30 minutes or more in the fridge.

To make the filling, fry the onion in the butter until soft. Add to the hot mashed potato, then add the cheese and mash till smooth. Season well, taste and allow to cool.

Roll out the dough on a floured surface to 3 mm (⅛ in) thick. Using a small glass, cut out rounds. Place on a floured tray and cover with a tea towel. Knead the scraps together and repeat making rounds until all the dough is used up.

Place a round in your palm and add a heaped teaspoon of the filling to the round. Fold the pastry over the filling. Pinch the edges together, first pinching in the middle, then pinching each side into the middle. Pinch again from end to end to create a firm seal.

Place the varenyky on a tea towel on a tray and cover with a tea towel. Keep making these soft little pillows.

In a large pot bring some salted water to the boil. Individually place 8–12 varenyky into the boiling water. Stir the water (not the varenyky) with the back of a wooden spoon. When they float to the surface, remove one or two with a slotted spoon and place flat on a tray to cool a little. Repeat the process.

To make the beurre noisette, melt the butter in a pan and boil until the foam dissipates and you are left with a hazelnut-brown colour and nutty smell. Set aside to cool.

Place the varenyky in a flattish shallow bowl and drizzle with the nut-coloured butter. Move these darlings carefully to coat them or they will stick together.

Serve the varenyky with sour cream and bacon or a splash of soy sauce if vegetarian.

Smachnoho! (Good appetite in Ukrainian.)

05

BREADS
and
CIRCUSES

'I WAS SO THIN I COULD SLICE BREAD WITH MY
SHOULDERBLADES, ONLY I SELDOM HAD BREAD.'
– CHARLES BUKOWSKI, THE LAST NIGHT
OF THE EARTH POEMS

MOTHER

The Mother is the life-force of bread, the soul and the essence. This slimy, wonderful mess gives bread the sourness and richness that's lost in supermarket bread. This living, breathing organism is unique to every household and environment, so look after it.

MOTHER

1 potato
4 tbsp live yoghurt
50 g (⅓ cup) wholemeal flour
100 g (⅔ cup) strong white flour
4 tbsp plain flour, plus extra for dusting

DAY 1

Grate the potato and mix with 210 ml (scant 1 cup) water and the yoghurt. Add the flours and stir until you have a wet, lumpy mixture. Place in a tall jar, dust with plain flour, cover with muslin cloth and leave somewhere warm (around 24–27°C/75–81°F).

DAY 2

Stir and dust with more flour.

DAY 3

Stir it again – you should see the mixture bubbling slightly. Add the plain flour and 4 tablespoons water, mix well and dust with more plain flour.

DAYS 4-5

On day 4, throw out about a third of the Mother and replace with all the mixture except for the potato. Repeat on day 5.

DAY 6

The Mother is ready to rock and should smell super sour and be active and bubbly.

After using, you will need to top it up with half flour and half water in equal measure to the amount of Mother you took out. Once replenished, leave for a day so it can go funky again.

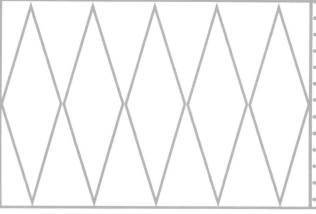

ROTI

MAKES 8 ROTI

If you feel lavish enough to make this, it's super worth it. No good curry should be served without roti, ever.

INGREDIENTS

300 g (2 cups) strong white bread flour
2 tsp sea salt
250 ml (1 cup) fridge-cold water
Plain flour, for dusting
100 g (⅓ cup) melted butter
60 ml (¼ cup) vegetable oil

METHOD

Combine the flour and salt in a large bowl. Make a well in the centre. Add the fridge-cold water and stir to combine. Use your hands to bring the dough together in the bowl.

Turn out onto a lightly floured surface and knead for 5 minutes or until smooth. Flatten the dough into a disc and cut into eight equal portions.

Shape each dough portion into a ball. Use a lightly floured rolling pin to roll out a portion of dough to a 20 cm (8 inch) diameter disc. Cover the remaining dough portions with plastic wrap.

Brush the disc with a little melted butter. Roll into a log to enclose the butter. Coil the dough into a scroll shape and flatten the scroll into a disc. Use a lightly floured rolling pin to roll out the disc until 15–20 cm (6–8 inches) in diameter. Repeat with the remaining dough portions.

Place a deep, heavy-based frying pan over medium-high heat and brush with a little oil. Cook one roti for 2 minutes each side or until puffed up and golden. Transfer to a serving platter and cover with a clean tea towel to keep warm. Repeat with the remaining roti.

FLAT BREADS

MAKES 8 FLAT BREADS

A staple at Africola and my personal favourite for soaking up drippings and gravy.

INGREDIENTS

250 ml (1 cup) lukewarm water
2 tsp active dry yeast
½ tsp sugar
35 g (¼ cup) wholemeal flour
300 g (2 cups) plain flour, plus extra
    for dusting
1 tsp sea salt
2 tbsp olive oil

METHOD

Put the lukewarm water in a large mixing bowl. Add the yeast and sugar and stir to dissolve. Add the wholemeal flour and 150 g (1 cup) of the plain flour and whisk together.

Put the bowl in a warm place, uncovered, for about 15 minutes until the mixture is frothy and bubbling.

Add the salt, olive oil and the remaining plain flour. Beat the mixture until it's incorporated. Dust with a little extra flour, then knead in the bowl for 1 minute, incorporating any stray bits of dry dough.

Turn the dough onto a floured work surface. Knead lightly for 2 minutes until smooth. Cover and let rest for 10 minutes, then knead again for 2 minutes. Try not to add too much extra flour; the dough should be soft and a bit moist.

Clean the mixing bowl and put the dough back in it. Cover the bowl tightly with plastic wrap, then cover with a tea towel. Put the bowl in a warm place and leave until the dough has doubled in size, about 1 hour.

Preheat the oven to 220°C (425°F).

On the bottom shelf of the oven, place a heavy-duty baking tray, large cast-iron pan or ceramic baking tile. Punch down the dough and divide into eight pieces of equal size. Form each piece into a little ball. Place the dough balls on the work surface, cover with a damp tea towel and leave for about 10 minutes.

Remove one ball (keeping the others covered) and press into a flat disc with a rolling pin. Roll to a 15 cm (6 inch) circle, then to a 20 cm (8 inch) diameter, about 3 mm (⅛ inch) thick, dusting with flour if necessary. (The dough will shrink a bit while baking.)

Carefully lift a dough circle and place quickly on the hot baking tray. After 2 minutes in the oven the dough should be nicely puffed. Turn over and bake for 1 minute more. The flat bread should be pale, with only a few brown speckles.

Transfer the warm flat bread to a napkin-lined basket and cover so the bread stays soft. Repeat with the rest of the dough balls.

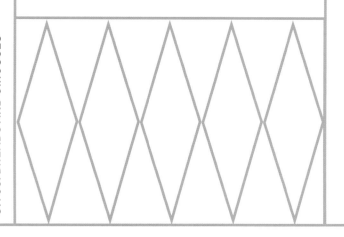

WHOLEMEAL LOAF

MAKES 4 LOAVES

We all know white bread is king, but there is something to be said about wholemeal bread with lashings of butter, pickled fish and cornichons or finely shaved Gouda, pickled onions and mustard. Where white bread is a vehicle for flavour, wholemeal bread provides something deeper, textural and wholesome, kind of like the difference between Britney Spears and Tori Amos.

INGREDIENTS

300 g (2 cups) strong wholemeal flour
200 g (1⅓ cups) strong white flour
½ tsp fresh yeast
100 g (3½ oz) Mother (page 172)
350 ml (scant 1½ cups) water, at
　room temperature
95 ml (generous ⅓ cup) fridge-cold water
25 g (scant ¼ cup) sea salt
Plain flour, for dusting

METHOD

Place the flours, yeast, Mother and room-temperature water in a mixer with a dough hook attachment and beat for 15 minutes, making sure everything is incorporated.

Leave to stand for 5 minutes, then pour in the fridge-cold water and the sea salt a little at a time until the dough is super smooth and all incorporated. Ball the dough and dust with plain flour, cover with a damp cloth and let prove for 1 hour.

Shape the dough into either batons or round loaves by rolling the dough flat, folding the dough in two and the ends in, and then turning it over, seam-side down. Score the dough and finish with another light dusting of flour. Leave for about 15 minutes until the loaves have doubled in size.

Preheat the oven to 230°C (450°F).

Bake the bread for about 30 minutes with a bowl of water at the base of the oven. After 30 minutes, take the bowl out, release some of the excess steam and bake for a further 10 minutes. To test the loaves for doneness, turn one over and tap on the base with your finger. If it sounds hollow, it's ready. Place on a wire rack to cool.

MILK BUNS

★ ★ ★

MAKES A BAKER'S DOZEN

Best buns for burgers. Now repeat this seven times really fast.

INGREDIENTS

350 ml (scant 1½ cups) milk
250 g (1 cup) unsalted butter, cut
  into pieces, plus extra for brushing
240 g (generous 1 cup) sugar
2¼ teaspoons active dry yeast
125 ml (½ cup) warm water
3 large eggs, lightly beaten
1½ teaspoons salt
1.4 kg (9½ cups) plain flour, plus extra
  for dusting
Sea salt, for sprinkling

METHOD

Place the milk in a small saucepan and bring to a simmer. Remove from the heat, stir in the butter and sugar and let cool.

Dissolve the yeast in the warm water and let sit until foamy.

Combine the milk mixture, eggs, yeast, salt and half of the flour in a mixer with the dough hook attachment and mix until smooth. Add the remaining flour, 75 g (½ cup) at a time, and stir until a smooth ball forms.

Remove the ball from the bowl and knead by hand on a floured surface for about 5 minutes. Place in a greased bowl, cover, and let rise in a warm place until doubled in bulk, about 60–70 minutes.

On a floured surface, punch down the dough, shape into small round balls and brush with a little melted butter and a sprinkle of sea salt. Place on a parchment-lined baking tray. Cover again and let rise until doubled in size, about 30–40 minutes.

Preheat the oven to 180°C (350°F).

Bake for 15–20 minutes or until golden and hollow sounding in the centre. Leave to cool on a wire rack.

WHITE BREAD

★ ★ ★

MAKES 4 LOAVES

Let's stop buggering about: white bread is
the number one flavour vehicle to soak up all
those pan juices, gravies and salad dressings.
Spread with some good butter, straight out of
the oven! Treat yourself.

INGREDIENTS

500 g (3⅓ cups) strong white flour
½ tsp fresh yeast
100 g (3½ oz) Mother (page 172)
350 ml (scant 1½ cups) water,
    at room temperature
75 ml (⅓ cup) fridge-cold water
1 tsp sea salt flakes
Plain flour, for dusting

METHOD

Place the flour, yeast, Mother and room-
temperature water in a mixer with a dough
hook attachment and beat for 15 minutes,
making sure everything is incorporated.

Leave to stand for 5 minutes, then pour in
the fridge-cold water and the sea salt a little
at a time until the dough is super smooth and
all incorporated.

Ball the dough and dust with plain flour,
cover with a damp cloth and prove for 1 hour.

Shape the dough into either batons or round
loaves by rolling the dough flat, folding the
dough in two and the ends in, and then
turning it over, seam-side down. Score the
dough and finish with another light dusting
of flour. Leave for about 15 minutes until the
loaves have doubled in size.

Preheat the oven to 230°C (450°F).

Bake the bread for about 30 minutes with a
bowl of water at the base of the oven. After
30 minutes, take the bowl out, release some
of the excess steam and bake for 10 minutes.

To test the loaves for doneness, turn one
over and tap on the base with your finger. If it
sounds hollow, it's ready. Place on a wire rack
to cool.

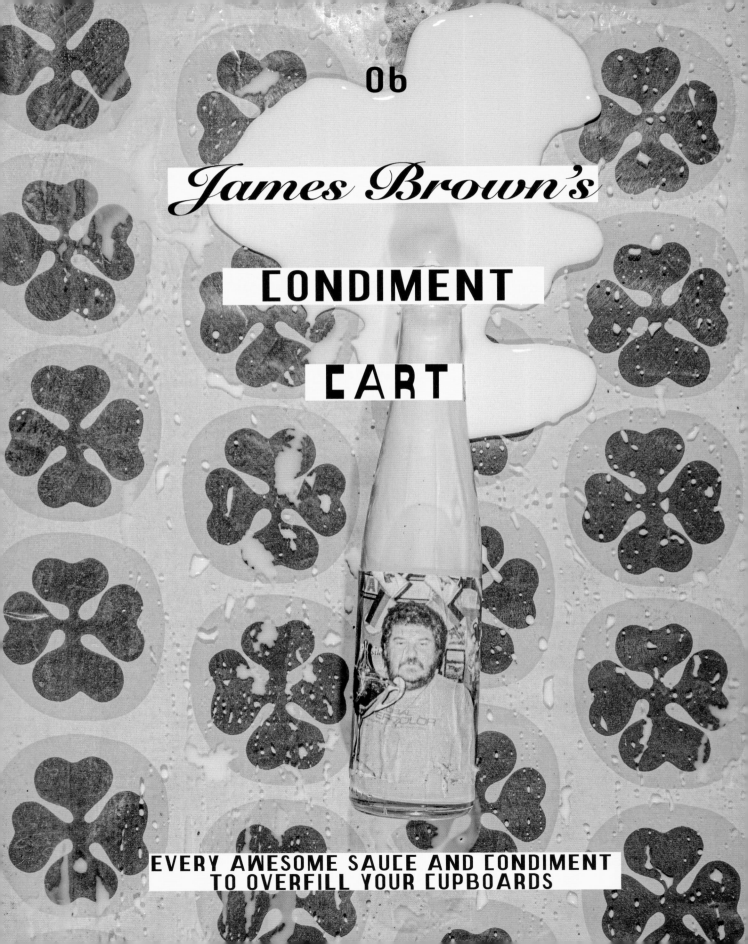

06

James Brown's

CONDIMENT

CART

EVERY AWESOME SAUCE AND CONDIMENT TO OVERFILL YOUR CUPBOARDS

Just another day contemplating a snack, in a world consisting of good folks vs. bad folks, all simply trying to make some smart decisions to win at the game. If you're bad and you want to get on a good foot, it's normally a state-of-mind adjustment broth that you seek, peace of mind and some afternoon delight. I've always found the quickest way to fix an ill brain salad or get someone into bed is not reaching into the cologne pantry, it's to get your ass on a plane or get your ass in the kitchen. And earthing thine knuckles on a chopping board is the cheapest of options – therapeutic repetition that brings together bowls of sustenance and survival for you and yours. Your shallot-laden tears with the stingle of habanero under them fingernails and onto your privates, if you didn't scrub proper, will remind you to keep your emotions in motion. Now, if you and your spicy privates can jump on a plane like a Bruce Lee Bourdain and roll your stone deep in the developing world where all the real street meats and island treats lurk, then you'll know the crux of good snacks vs. bad snacks really lives and dies on one thing ... the condiments applied.

Sometimes a multitude. So you need to arm up. A two-step program, which will 110 per cent have the Joneses peeping over the fence in envious lust and potentially have you sewing alfalfa sprouts into your hot neighbour's couch when their spouse is away on business. It calls for three fridges. One for food, one for booze, one for weapons of mass adornment. So is born your James Brown's Condiment Fridge to support your <insert name here> Condiment Cart.

With our favourite mayos, salsas, sambals, mustards, atchars, sauces, vinegars, jellies, relishes, dippy dippers and hallucinogenic potions we bring you the chapter that is the most important of them all. Fuck this Welgemoed with his tweezers, poor man's caviar tricks and fancy vegetables. Here's my bagged, boxed and bottled collection of thirty-five superfragilistic kung fu zingers stolen and reconstituted to spice up many a good, bad or downright ugly broth. Don't leave home without them.

Le Godfather of Sauce

James Ye-ha Brown

AMERICAN-STYLE HOT CHILLI BOY

MAKES 2 LITRES (70 FL OZ)

INGREDIENTS

1 kg (2 lb 4 oz) red chillies
  (use cayenne or tabasco)
3 tbsp sea salt
500 ml (2 cups) filtered water
250 ml (1 cup) apple cider vinegar

EQUIPMENT

Spice mill, coffee grinder or mortar
  and pestle

METHOD

First, ferment the chillies. Blend your fresh chillies in a food processor with ½ tablespoon of the salt. Tip into a few sterilised jars, leaving at least 2–3 cm (1 inch) of headspace.

Next, mix together the water and remaining sea salt. Pour just enough of this brine over the chillies to cover them, pressing them down a bit as you go. It is important to keep the chillies covered with brine to avoid spoilage. Check this daily.

Screw on the lids and set the jars away from direct sunlight to ferment for at least 1 week. The ideal temperature is between 15–20°C (59–68°F) and the most active fermentation period is between 1–2 weeks, so be sure to monitor them during this time. 'Burp' the jars often by unscrewing the lids a bit to let out some of the accumulating gases.

After 1–2 weeks, the fermenting activity will diminish and the brine will turn cloudy and taste acidic.

Pour the fermented peppers, including the brine, into a pan along with the vinegar. Bring to a quick boil. Reduce the heat and simmer for 15 minutes.

Cool slightly, then add to a food processor and process until smooth.

Strain the mixture to remove the solids. Spoon into sterilised jars. The chilli sauce will keep for 6 months unharmed.

AMAYONNAISING ★ MAYO

MAKES 300 G (10½ OZ)

INGREDIENTS

2 tbsp rice vinegar
5 tsp malt vinegar
1 tsp sea salt
½ tsp MSG
½ tsp Japanese mustard powder
⅛ tsp dashi powder
⅛ tsp garlic powder
2 large egg yolks
250 ml (1 cup) vegetable oil

METHOD

Whisk together the rice and malt vinegars, salt, MSG, mustard, dashi and garlic powders in a small bowl until completely dissolved.

Place the vinegar mixture in a food processor with the egg yolks. Pulse to combine. With the motor running, slowly drizzle in the vegetable oil in a thin, steady stream until all combined. Transfer the mayonnaise to an airtight container and store in the fridge for up to 2 weeks.

BLACK MUSTARD

MAKES 200 G (7 OZ)

INGREDIENTS

6 tbsp yellow mustard seeds
100 g (⅔ cup) black mustard seeds
2 tsp sea salt flakes
2 tbsp honey
150 ml (scant ⅔ cup) Guinness
60 ml (¼ cup) balsamic vinegar
2 tbsp sherry vinegar

EQUIPMENT

Spice mill, coffee grinder or mortar
  and pestle

METHOD

Grind the mustard seeds for a few seconds
in a spice mill or coffee grinder or by hand
with a mortar and pestle until fine.

Pour the ground seeds into a bowl and add
the salt and honey.

Pour in the beer, then stir well. When
everything is incorporated, let this sit for
up to 10 minutes. The longer you let it sit,
the mellower the mustard will be. When
you're ready, pour in the vinegars.

Pour into a sterilised glass jar and store in
the fridge. It will be runny at first. Don't
worry, it will thicken up overnight. Wait
for at least 12 hours before using. Mustard
made this way will last for a year in
the fridge.

SMOKED FISH SAUCE

MAKES 4 LITRES (135 FL OZ)

INGREDIENTS

1 litre (4 cups) filtered water
3 litres (12 cups) fish sauce
1 kg (2 lb 4 oz) light palm sugar (jaggery)
Aromatic scraps – lemongrass,
  galangal, chilli, lime leaf

EQUIPMENT

Stainless steel saucepan
Charcoal barbecue
Hickory smoking chips, soaked
  in water overnight

METHOD

Place all the ingredients in a stainless
steel pan, bring to the boil and simmer
for 5–10 minutes or until the flavour is
salty and sweet and the aromatics have
steeped enough to taste them. Let cool.

Set up your barbecue with a very low
fire and wait until the coals have ashed
over. Place the hickory smoking chips
on the coals, then place the pan on a
wire grill above the barbecue, cover and
smoke for 5 minutes.

Strain the fish mulch after 6 months and
spoon into sterilised bottles. This will
keep for another 6 months, refrigerated.

DUCK ★ SAUCE

MAKES 600 G (1 LB 5 OZ)

INGREDIENTS

80 ml (⅓ cup) soy sauce
2 tbsp smooth peanut butter
1 tbsp dark brown sugar
2 tsp rice vinegar
1 garlic clove, finely minced
2 tsp sesame oil
1 tsp hot sauce, to taste
⅛ tsp freshly ground black pepper

METHOD

Add all the ingredients to a blender and blitz until smooth.

Serve with crispy duck.

MILLION ISLAND SAUCE

MAKES 280 ML (9½ FL OZ)

INGREDIENTS

250 ml (1 cup) mayonnaise
2 spring onions (scallions), minced
2 tbsp ketchup
1 tsp lemon juice
½ tsp sweet paprika
¼ tsp sea salt
2 tsp sweet chilli sauce

METHOD

Combine all the ingredients in a small mixing bowl and whisk until emulsified. This sauce will keep for 2–3 days in a plastic container in the fridge.

KETCHUP

MAKES 600 G (1 LB 5 OZ)

INGREDIENTS

400 g (14 oz) tin plum tomatoes

1 onion, chopped

4 garlic cloves, chopped

2 tbsp vegetable oil

¼ tsp sea salt

1 tsp chilli powder

½ tsp paprika

¼ tsp ground cinnamon

¼ tsp ground allspice

½ tsp freshly ground black pepper

1 tbsp tomato paste (concentrated purée)

110 g (½ cup) packed light brown sugar

125 ml (½ cup) cider vinegar

METHOD

Purée the tomatoes with their juices in a blender until smooth.

Cook the onion and garlic in the oil with the salt in a heavy saucepan over medium heat for about 8 minutes, stirring occasionally, until golden.

Add the spices and pepper and cook, stirring frequently, for 1 minute. Add the tomato paste, brown sugar and vinegar and simmer, uncovered and stirring occasionally, for 45–55 minutes until very thick. Stir more frequently towards the end of the cooking time to prevent scorching.

Purée the ketchup in the blender until smooth (use caution when blending hot liquids). Chill for at least 2 hours for the flavours to develop.

Spoon into sterilised jars. Will store for up to 6 months unopened in a cool, dark place ... like my heart.

SAVOURY TREACLE
★ ★ ★
MAKES 250 G (9 OZ)

INGREDIENTS

1 litre (4 cups) brewer's yeast
300 ml (1¼ cups) filtered water
1 onion, diced
2 carrots, diced
1 turnip, diced
2 leeks, white part only, diced
½ celery stick, diced
2 garlic cloves, roughly chopped
80 g (3 oz) fresh ginger, peeled
  and diced
Pinch of sea salt
1 star anise

EQUIPMENT

Cooking thermometer
Bain marie
Muslin cloth

METHOD

Blend the brewer's yeast, water, vegetables, garlic, ginger and salt until as smooth as your blender allows, then transfer to a bain marie.

Simmer with the star anise at blood heat (30–40°C/86–104°F) for 10 hours or overnight. Next, simmer at 50–60°C (122–140°F) for 2–3 hours. Finally, boil at 90°C (194°F) for 30 minutes.

Filter the mix through muslin cloth into a sterilised jar. Let it cool for a day or so. It will separate further. Filter again.

You now want to convert the mix to a paste. This is best achieved by putting it in a large flat pan and simmering – kind of like making hashish. As it simmers, it will reduce and look like a demi-glace or treacle. Once this is achieved, spoon into sterilised jars.

The yeast extract will keep for about 7 million years, or at least until governments all around the world are in total unison acknowledging that we are in a climate crisis. Tastes great on toast or as an enricher in stews and gravies.

MANGO AND HABANERO HOT SAUCE

MAKES ABOUT 1 SMALL JAR

INGREDIENTS

8 habanero chillies, stems removed

2 French shallots

100 g (3½ oz) mango flesh

3 garlic cloves

1 tsp ground cumin

Juice of 6 limes

2 tbsp apple cider vinegar

Sea salt

METHOD

Blend everything together in a food processor or blender. Taste and season with salt, if needed.

Pour into a sterilised glass jar, seal and keep refrigerated for up to 2 weeks.

185

SPICY PEANUT DIPPING SAUCE

This a great dipping sauce for grilled pork skewers or even grilled bananas.

MAKES 300 ML (10½ FL OZ)

INGREDIENTS

1 tbsp peanut oil
2 garlic cloves, crushed
2 red Asian shallots, finely chopped
4 small red chillies, thinly sliced
140 g (½ cup) smooth peanut butter
250 ml (1 cup) light coconut milk
60 ml (¼ cup) kecap manis
1 tbsp Worcestershire sauce
2 tsp light soy sauce
40 g (¼ cup) crushed unsalted
  roasted peanuts
Juice of 1 lime

EQUIPMENT

High-speed blender or smoothie maker

METHOD

Literally chuck everything in a high-speed blender or smoothie maker and blitz on high for 2 minutes.

EAT WITH COLD VEGETABLES
AND BOILED MEATS

ANCHOVY SAUCE

MAKES 300 ML (10½ FL OZ)

INGREDIENTS

Juice and zest of 1 lemon
125 ml (½ cup) extra virgin olive oil
55 g (2 oz) good-quality anchovy fillets
4 garlic cloves, finely chopped
Pinch of ground chilli
2½ tbsp extra virgin olive oil
180 ml (¾ cup) single (pure) cream
Sea salt and freshly ground black pepper
Bread rolls, to serve (just plain white,
  something to mop up the juices)

EQUIPMENT

High-speed blender or smoothie maker

METHOD

Blitz all the ingredients except the cream in a high-speed blender or smoothie maker.

Slowly add the cream and just a little warm water to help emulsify the dressing.

RANCHO RELAXO

DRESSIN'

MAKES 500 ML (17 FL OZ)

INGREDIENTS

200 g (generous ¾ cup) mayonnaise
100 g (scant ½ cup) sour cream
100 ml (scant ½ cup) buttermilk
1 tsp chopped dill
½ tsp chopped flat-leaf parsley
½ tsp chopped chives
¼ tsp onion powder
½ tsp garlic powder
¼ tsp fine sea salt
⅛ tsp finely ground white pepper
1–3 tsp freshly squeezed lemon juice,
   or to taste

METHOD

Whisk together the mayo, sour cream and buttermilk until smooth. Add the herbs, onion and garlic powders and then the salt and pepper and whisk until combined.

Add the lemon juice and whisk again, then pour into a jar and chill in the fridge until ready to serve. Will keep for a week.

PEPPER VINEGAR SAUCE AKA GOOD-FOR-THE-GUT SPICY DRANK

MAKES 1 LITRE (35 FL OZ)

INGREDIENTS

1 litre (4 cups) kombucha vinegar
   or any raw vinegar
250 g (9 oz) scud chillies
4 garlic cloves
1 tbsp whole black peppercorns

EQUIPMENT

1 litre (35 fl oz) sterilised glass
   bottle with a cap

METHOD

In a non-reactive saucepan, bring enough vinegar to fill your bottle to a simmer, being careful not to boil.

While the vinegar is heating, set aside enough chillies to fill the bottle. You may remove the stems if you prefer, but it's not necessary.

Using a knife, make a small slit in each of the chillies and add to the bottle. This slit allows the vinegar to more easily penetrate the chillies and soak up their goodness. Smash the garlic cloves and add those along with the peppercorns.

Fill the sterilised bottle with the heated vinegar. Will keep for at least 6 months in the bottle in a cool, dark place.

187

ASK DUNCAN'S MUM

SEAWEED XO
Pg. 192

AFRICOLA CURE-ALL TAHINI SAUCE
Pg. 195

MARY'S BURGER BEER
CHEESE SAUCE
Pg. 196

PLUM CHUTNEY

MAKES 600 G (1 LB 5 OZ)

INGREDIENTS

1 star anise
1 whole clove
5 cm (2 inch) piece of cinnamon stick
150 ml (scant ⅔ cup) red wine vinegar
100 g (½ cup) sugar
5 cm (2 inch) piece of fresh ginger, peeled and cut into 1 cm (½ inch) thick rounds
1 tbsp yellow mustard seeds
1 tsp freshly ground black pepper
1.5 kg (3 lb 5 oz) plums
Sea salt

EQUIPMENT

Spice mill, coffee grinder or mortar and pestle

METHOD

Finely grind the star anise, clove and cinnamon stick together in a spice mill, coffee grinder or by hand using a mortar and pestle.

Combine the spice mixture, vinegar, sugar, ginger, mustard seeds and pepper in a large heavy saucepan. Stir over medium–high heat until the sugar dissolves and bring to the boil.

Add the plums, reduce the heat to low, cover and simmer for about 30 minutes, stirring occasionally, until the chutney thickens and a chunky sauce forms. Cool. Season to taste with salt.

Spoon into sterilised jars. The chutney will keep for 6 months in a cool, dark place.

SPOON OVER GRILLED LAMB OR BEEF.

MINT JELLY

MAKES ENOUGH FOR 4–5 SMALL JARS

INGREDIENTS

1 kg (2 lb 4 oz) Granny Smith apples
125 ml (½ cup) lemon juice
250 g (9 oz) mint leaves, plus 20 extra leaves, finely chopped
150 g (⅔ cup) sugar (approx.)

EQUIPMENT

Muslin cloth

METHOD

Cut the apples into thick slices, but do not peel or core.

Combine the apples, 1 litre (4 cups) water, the lemon juice and mint leaves in a large saucepan. Bring to the boil and cook for 10 minutes until the apples are soft.

Strain the apple mixture through a muslin cloth-lined sieve over a bowl and let it stand overnight.

Measure the strained juice and return to a large, clean saucepan. Add 1 cup sugar for each cup of juice and stir over medium heat until the sugar is dissolved.

Bring to the boil and boil rapidly for 15 minutes or until the setting point is reached. Test this by placing a small plate in the fridge to get cold. Take out and spoon a bit of the liquid onto the plate. When it sets, you're ready to go. Remove from the heat and add the chopped mint leaves.

Allow to stand for 10 minutes and stir the mint through to disperse evenly. Pour into sterilised jars. The mint jelly will keep for at least 3 Boxing Days.

NAM JIM

THALEH

MAKES ENOUGH TO NEVER
BUY THE SAUCE AGAIN

INGREDIENTS

100 g (3½ oz) scud chillies
80 g (3 oz) peeled garlic cloves
1 bunch of coriander (cilantro), leaves
   and roots finely chopped
100 g (½ cup) palm sugar (jaggery)
150 ml (scant ⅔ cup) fish sauce
300 ml (1¼ cups) lime juice
400 g (14 oz) cherry tomatoes,
   quartered

EQUIPMENT

Mortar and pestle

METHOD

Pound the chillies, garlic, coriander
leaves and roots in a mortar and pestle
to a coarse paste, then add the palm
sugar and pound so the paste is thick
and soft.

Add the liquids and balance the
sweetness, saltiness and sourness a
little at a time and to your taste. Finish
by folding in the tomatoes. Don't keep
for more than a few days. Kidding.

★ ★ ★

SOY BOY SOUS

MAKES 6 X 1 LITRE (35 FL OZ) BOTTLES

INGREDIENTS

500 g (1 lb 2 oz) high-quality soya beans
350 g (2⅓ cups) plain flour
4 litres (16 cups) filtered water
200 g (1½ cups) sea salt

EQUIPMENT

Muslin cloth

METHOD

Cook the soya beans in boiling salted water
for 2 hours or until soft. Drain, add to a
food processor and blend to a paste.

Pour the puréed beans into a bowl and
combine with the flour, then tip the mixture
onto a clean surface and shape into a log.
Cut the log into 5 mm (¼ inch) thick slices.

Arrange the slices on a moist paper towel
and cover with another wet paper towel.
Cover in plastic wrap and put away in a
dark, cool place. Allow to sit for 7 days or
until the discs are covered in mould.

Unwrap the discs and arrange them on a
baking tray so they do not touch. Leave
them to dry for roughly 12 hours in direct
sunlight (they should turn brown when dry).

Pour the water and salt into a large pot or
tall bucket, stirring to combine. Add the
discs, cover with a lid and store in a cool,
dark place.

Dissolve the discs in the salt water, which
can take up to 6 months, stirring daily.
When dissolved, strain through a muslin
cloth and bottle in sterilised bottles. The
sauce will keep for a year or more.

SEAWEED

XO

Seaweed XO is an excellent sauce to dress green things, meat things, shellfish things and all inanimate objects, alive or dead.

MAKES 280 ML (GENEROUS 1 CUP)

INGREDIENTS

8 g (¼ oz) shrimp paste
50 g (2 oz) dried scallops or abalone
75 g (2 oz) dried prawns
100 g (3½ oz) dried kombu
250 ml (1 cup) vegetable oil, or just
　　enough to cover all the ingredients
100 g (3½ oz) garlic (about 20 cloves),
　　finely chopped
6 red Asian shallots, finely chopped
65 g (2½ oz) smoked bacon, chopped
　　into lardons
6 long red chillies, seeded and
　　finely chopped
2 dried long red chillies, seeded,
　　soaked until softened and
　　finely chopped
100 g (3½ oz) toasted nori
5 dried bird's eye chillies,
　　finely chopped
2 tbsp dried shrimp roe, crumbled
　　(optional)
2 tbsp sugar, or to taste
Pinch of sea salt

METHOD

Toast the shrimp paste by wrapping in foil and roasting in a hot oven for 10 minutes.

Soak the scallops, prawns and kombu separately in 125 ml (½ cup) hot water each until plump (preferably overnight).

Drain the scallops (reserve the soaking water), tear them into fine shreds, pat dry on paper towel and set aside. Drain the prawns (reserve the water), chop them finely and set aside. Drain the kombu, finely chop and set aside.

Heat half the oil in a wok or large saucepan over medium–high heat, add the scallops and deep-fry for 1–2 minutes (cover with a lid as they may spit) until very crisp. Drain well, reserving the oil. Wipe out the wok with paper towel, add the reserved oil and remaining fresh oil and return to medium heat.

Add the garlic, shallots and dried prawns and stir continuously for 4–5 minutes until golden brown.

Add the bacon, fresh chilli and dried chilli and fry for a few seconds (be careful, it burns easily), then add the shrimp paste, fried scallops and reserved scallop and prawn water and stir continuously for a few more seconds.

Add the remaining ingredients and cook, stirring occasionally, for 20–30 minutes until fragrant and the water has completely evaporated. Remove from the heat and strain, reserving the oil. Transfer the solids to a sterilised jar, then pour in enough reserved oil to cover. XO sauce will keep refrigerated in a sealed container for 1 month.

SAUCE PIL PIL

MAKES 150 ML (5 FL OZ)

INGREDIENTS

10 shell-on prawns, peeled but heads
  left on
100 ml (scant ½ cup) Hellfire oil
  (see opposite)
10 garlic cloves, finely sliced
2 tsp crushed dried chillies
3 sprigs of curly parsley, roughly chopped
½ tsp sweet paprika
Juice of 2 lemons
Splash of Pepper vinegar sauce (page 187)
Sea salt

EQUIPMENT

Charcoal barbecue
Earthenware casserole dish
High-speed blender

METHOD

Light the charcoal in your barbecue and
when the coals have ashed, place the
prawns on a wire grill over the barbecue
and cook until they are nice and pink. Set
aside in a bowl to reserve all the juices.

Add the hellfire oil to an earthenware
casserole dish over a high flame. When the
oil is hot, add the garlic, chilli, parsley and
paprika and cook for 2 minutes.

Once all these ingredients are sweated,
incorporate the prawns and their juices,
take off the heat and leave to rest for a few
minutes. Deglaze the dish with the lemon
juice and the white pepper sauce and
season with salt.

Take the prawn heads and squeeze out all
the juices into the sauce, discarding the
shells. Blend everything in a high-speed
blender, then check the seasoning, pass
through a sieve and try not drink the
whole lot in one go.

HELLFIRE OIL

MAKES 1.5 LITRES (6 CUPS)

This recipe was shamelessly stolen
from Chin Chin's Ben Cooper, who
stole it from someone, who stole it
from someone, and so on and so forth.
You can also add dried spices or
toasted coconut to this for variance.
This is perfect to replace oils in
dressings to spice things up.

INGREDIENTS

350 g (12 oz) dried Thai red chillies
300 g (10½ oz) garlic cloves, peeled
200 g (7 oz) homemade deep-fried
  French shallots, oil reserved
  (follow the method on page 203
  for frying garlic)
100 g (scant ½ cup) caster sugar
50 g (scant ½ cup) sea salt
500 ml (2 cups) shallot oil (from the
  deep-fried shallots)
500 ml (2 cups) garlic oil
100 ml (scant ½ cup) fish sauce

EQUIPMENT

Mortar and pestle

METHOD

Pound the chillies, garlic, deep-fried
shallots, sugar and salt into a paste in
a mortar and pestle.

Add to a saucepan with the shallot and
garlic oils and the fish sauce and bring
up to the boil, then set aside, stirring
to dissolve the sugar and salt. Allow
to sit overnight before using. Will keep
forever.

CURRYWURST SAUCE

MAKES 550 ML (2¼ CUPS)

INGREDIENTS

2 tbsp canola oil
1 large onion, finely chopped
1 tbsp curry powder
1 tbsp hot paprika
400 g (14 oz) tin plum tomatoes
100 g (½ cup) sugar
80 ml (⅓ cup) red wine vinegar
Sea salt, to taste

METHOD

Heat the oil in a saucepan over medium heat. Add the onion and cook for about 10 minutes until soft.

Add the curry powder and hot paprika. Cook for 1 minute more.

Using your hands, crush the tinned tomatoes with their juices into the pan.

Add the sugar, red wine vinegar and salt, to taste, and stir well. Increase the heat to high and bring to the boil.

Reduce the heat to medium–low and simmer for about 25 minutes, stirring occasionally, until thickened.

The sauce will keep in a plastic container in the fridge for up to 2 weeks.

BREX-IT

SAUCE

MAKES 2 SMALL JARS

INGREDIENTS

500 g (1 lb 2 oz) pitted dates
1 onion, chopped
2 garlic cloves, chopped
1 chilli, seeded and chopped
Juice of 1 orange
75 ml (scant ⅓ cup) apple juice
Pinch of mace
Pinch of ground allspice
75 ml (scant ⅓ cup) malt vinegar
50 g (2 oz) molasses
50 g (2 oz) tamarind paste
25 g (1 oz) tomato paste
  (concentrated purée)
150 ml (scant ⅔ cup) filtered
  cold water
1 tsp sea salt

METHOD

Put all the ingredients in a large saucepan. Cover the surface with baking parchment. Simmer over low heat for 50 minutes until the dates soften. Cool for 30 minutes.

Transfer the mixture to a blender and blend, then decant into two sterilised jars while warm. Seal and store in the fridge. Will keep for up to 2 months.

SRIRACHACHACHA

Spicy and tangy and makes a terrible and suspicious vehicle to store meth in.

MAKES 3 LITRES (100 FL OZ)

INGREDIENTS

2 kg (4 lb 8 oz) scud chillies
3 tbsp sea salt
500 ml (2 cups) filtered water
100 ml (scant ½ cup) fish sauce
4 garlic cloves, chopped
3 tbsp light brown sugar
1 tsp sugar
250 ml (1 cup) rice vinegar

METHOD

First, ferment the chillies. Blend your chillies in a food processor. If you don't have a processor, use a mortar and pestle or finely chop. Pack into a few sterilised jars with half the salt, leaving at least 2–3 cm (1 inch) of headspace.

Next, mix the water with the rest of the salt. Pour just enough of this brine over the chillies to cover, pressing them down a bit as you go. It is important to keep the chillies covered with brine to avoid spoilage.

Screw on the lids and set the jars away from direct sunlight to ferment for at least 1 week. The ideal temperature is about 26°C (79°F) and the most active fermentation period is 1–2 weeks, so be sure to check them daily during this time. 'Burp' the jars often by unscrewing the lids a bit to let out some of the accumulating gases.

After 1–2 weeks, the fermenting activity will diminish and the brine will turn cloudy and taste acidic.

Pour the fermented chillies, including the brine, into a pan along with the fish sauce, garlic, sugars and vinegar. Bring to a quick boil. Reduce the heat and simmer for 5–10 minutes.

Cool slightly, then process in a food processor until smooth. Strain the mixture to remove the solids. Spoon into sterilised jars and store somewhere cool and dark.

AFRICOLA CURE-ALL TAHINI SAUCE

MAKES 200 ML (7 FL OZ)

INGREDIENTS

1 garlic clove, crushed
150 g (generous ½ cup) tahini paste
2 tsp white wine vinegar
Juice of 2 lemons
¼ tsp ground cumin
50 g (1 cup) chopped flat-leaf parsley

METHOD

Combine the garlic, tahini and vinegar in a bowl, then whisk in the lemon juice and 125 ml (½ cup) cold water to form a creamy sauce. Stir in the cumin and parsley.

The tahini sauce will keep for 2–3 days in a plastic container in the fridge. (Not too long as the acid won't be as pronounced and the herbs will oxidise.)

MARY'S BURGER BEER CHEESE SAUCE

Shown to me by Jake Smythe of Mary's, one of my best friends and bad influences. You cannot fuck with the Mary's burger. It beats every burger I have ever eaten. I don't have the recipe for it in here unfortunately, but here's the cheese sauce.

MAKES 2 LITRES (70 FL OZ)

INGREDIENTS

1 litre (4 cups) lager
1 kg (2 lb 4 oz) Kraft singles

METHOD

Bring the beer to the boil, add the cheese and whisk until emulsified.

Pour over tater tots or over a burger.

Die.

GREAT AS A SIDE TO SERVE WITH
HOT CURRIES OR GRILLED MEATS.

PICKLED TURMERIC

MAKES 600 ML (2⅓ CUPS)

INGREDIENTS

250 g (9 oz) peeled garlic cloves, pounded
  to a rough paste
250 g (9 oz) fresh peeled turmeric, pounded
  to a rough paste
30 g (¼ cup) sea salt
150 g (⅔ cup) caster sugar
350 ml (scant 1½ cups) rice vinegar
2 large red chillies, roughly chopped
2 large green chillies, roughly chopped

METHOD

Mix all of the ingredients together. Place in a stainless steel pan, bring to the boil and simmer for 2–3 minutes. Remove from the heat and allow to cool. Will keep in the fridge in a plastic container for a few weeks.

WORCESTER-SHER-SHIRE SAUCE

MAKES ENOUGH TO NEVER BUY THE SAUCE AGAIN

MAKES 2 LITRES (70 FL OZ)

INGREDIENTS

4 litres (16 cups) malt vinegar
1 garlic bulb, cloves peeled
1 tsp sea salt
1 tsp ground allspice
½ tsp ground nutmeg
½ tsp ground cloves
¼ tsp freshly ground black pepper
500 ml (2 cups) treacle
440 g (15½ oz) plum jam
1 red bird's eye chilli

METHOD

Place all the ingredients into a large saucepan. Bring to the boil, lower the heat and simmer for 1 hour.

Allow to cool to room temperature. Strain through a fine sieve.

Bottle in sterilised bottles and store for 2 weeks before using. Will keep for a year at least.

SOMEONE'S

NONNA'S RED SAUCE

MAKES 500 ML (2 CUPS)

INGREDIENTS

150 ml (generous ½ cup) extra
   virgin olive oil
2 white onions, finely sliced
4 garlic cloves, chopped
½ tbsp salt
¼ tsp freshly ground black pepper
25 g (1 oz) dried porcini
Large pinch of chilli flakes
750 g (1 lb 10 oz) fresh tomatoes
3 x 400 g (14 oz) tins chopped tomatoes
1 small handful of oregano,
   finely chopped
5 large basil leaves
Pinch of caster sugar, if necessary

METHOD

Heat half the oil in a large saucepan and sweat the onion, garlic, salt, pepper, porcini and chilli over medium heat for about 15 minutes.

When transparent, add the fresh tomatoes and the rest of the oil and cook over low–medium heat for 15 minutes. Add the tinned tomatoes and bring to a gentle simmer. Leave to bubble on the lowest heat for about 1 hour.

Turn off the heat and add the oregano and basil. Taste and see if it needs any sugar. When you're pleased with the taste, whiz together with a blender.

This sauce will keep in the fridge for a week and freezes beautifully too.

SOY BOY SOUS
Pg. 191

MINT JELLY
Pg. 190

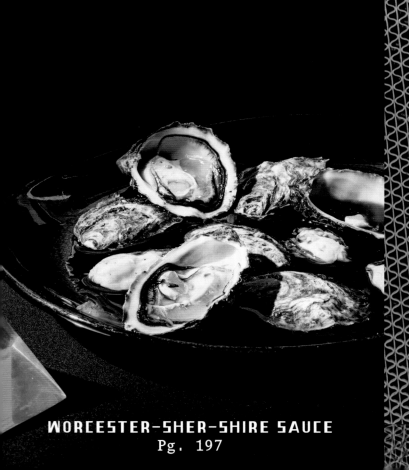

WORCESTER-SHER-SHIRE SAUCE
Pg. 197

RANCHO RELAXO DRESSIN'
Pg. 187

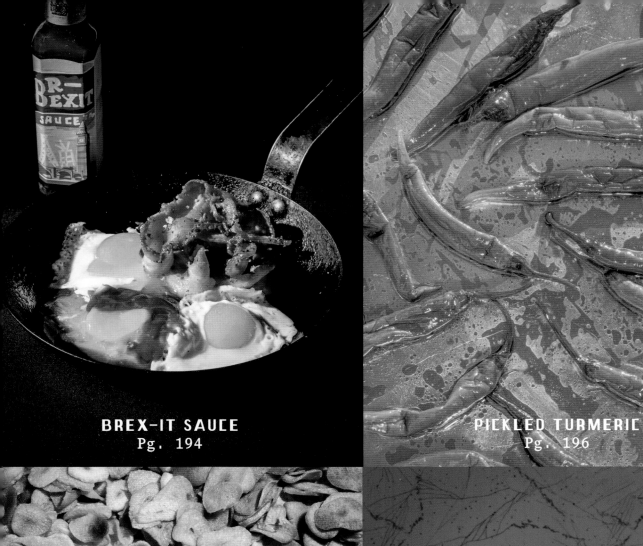

BREX-IT SAUCE
Pg. 194

PICKLED TURMERIC
Pg. 196

FRIED GARLIC
Pg. 203

SOMEONE'S NONNA'S RED SAUCE
Pg. 197

CHIMICHURRI

My favourite steak sauce. Really good with steamed or raw vegetables as well.

MAKES 250 G (9 OZ)

INGREDIENTS

150 g (2½ cups) coarsely chopped
  flat-leaf parsley
60 ml (¼ cup) red wine vinegar
5 tbsp kimchi juice
4 large garlic cloves, minced
2 tbsp oregano leaves
2 tsp dried chillies
200 ml (generous ¾ cup) extra
  virgin olive oil
Sea salt and freshly ground
  black pepper

METHOD

In a food processor, combine the parsley, vinegar, kimchi juice, garlic, oregano and dried chillies. Process until smooth and season with salt and pepper. Transfer the sauce to a bowl and pour the olive oil over the mixture. Let stand for at least 20 minutes.

Keep in a glass jar for no more than a week.

THE SWEETNESS FOR OUR ROAST CAULIFLOWER (PAGE 104).

FIG AND PISTACHIO AGRODOLCE

MAKES 500 G (1 LB 2 OZ)

INGREDIENTS

2½ tbsp red wine vinegar
2 tbsp chopped dried figs
2 tbsp extra virgin olive oil
1 French shallot, thinly sliced
3 garlic cloves, finely chopped
400 g (14 oz) tin cherry tomatoes
½ tsp brown sugar
2 tbsp pistachio nuts, toasted
Sea salt and freshly ground black pepper

EQUIPMENT

Small non-reactive bowl

METHOD

Combine the vinegar and figs in a small non-reactive bowl and set aside for about 10–15 minutes until the figs are plump.

Heat a large frying pan over medium heat, add half the oil and all the shallot and garlic and cook, stirring occasionally, for 7–10 minutes until soft. Add the tomatoes and cook, stirring occasionally, for 5–7 minutes until thick. Add the sugar, pistachios, figs and vinegar, stir, bring to the boil and cook for 10 minutes. Season to taste and set aside. This will keep in the fridge for 2–3 weeks in a sterilised jar.

BAGNA CAUDA

★ ★ ★

MAKES 150 ML (5 FL OZ)

INGREDIENTS

125 ml (½ cup) extra virgin olive oil
8 garlic cloves, crushed
20 Spanish anchovies preserved in
 olive oil, drained and chopped
120 g (½ cup) unsalted butter, cut
 into cubes
80 ml (⅓ cup) thick (double) cream

METHOD

Put the olive oil in a frying pan with
the garlic and anchovies and stir over
low heat for a few minutes. Whisk in
90 g (3¼ oz) of the butter and, as soon
as it has melted, remove from the heat
and whisk a few more times so that
everything is creamy and amalgamated.

Taste, and if you feel you want this
dipping sauce – which is meant to
be pungent but not acrid – a little
more mellow, then whisk in 2 more
tablespoons butter.

Whisk in the cream. Serve.

NAM PRIK

MAKES ABOUT 1 SMALL JAR

This is great for dressing raw fish and
thinly sliced beef or it makes a brilliant
dressing for thinly sliced raw vegetables
and exotic fruits.

INGREDIENTS

115 g (⅔ cup) palm sugar (jaggery),
 coarsely chopped
60 ml (¼ cup) Thai fish sauce
30 g (1 oz) seedless tamarind pulp (paste)
1 tbsp cayenne pepper
3–4 scud chillies, chopped
2½ tbsp lime juice

METHOD

Combine the palm sugar, fish sauce,
tamarind pulp and 300 ml (1¼ cups) water
in a pan. Set over high heat, bring the
mixture to boil, then immediately reduce
the heat to maintain a simmer.

Use a whisk or spoon to break up the palm
sugar and tamarind pulp as they soften and
cook for about 5–8 minutes, just until the
tamarind has fully softened and dissolved
into the mixture.

Stir in the cayenne, chillies and lime, turn
off the heat, and let the mixture sit, stirring
occasionally, until it has cooled to room
temperature. Use immediately or refrigerate
for up to a week in sterilised bottles.

SARON GAS SALSA

This is a salsa I made for school kids in Oaxaca. They didn't believe a gringo could make salsa or play soccer. I showed them*. The name comes from my second cousin twice-removed's old band. His band is now called Seether. Love you Shaun.

*Most kids don't like spicy foods so they hardly ate it. They also beat me at soccer. The salsa was fucking delicious though.

MAKES 500 ML (2 CUPS)

INGREDIENTS

4 plum tomatoes
10 scud chillies
12 guajillo chillies
5 chipotle morita chillies or any
  hot dried chillies
½ tsp dried Mexican oregano
¼ tsp cumin seeds
10 garlic cloves, skins on
2½ tsp sea salt
2 tbsp sugar
1 tbsp distilled vinegar
1 tbsp lemon juice

EQUIPMENT

Charcoal barbecue
Large cast-iron pan
Spice mill, coffee grinder or mortar
  and pestle

METHOD

Light your barbecue and wait until the coals have ashed over. Roast the tomatoes and fresh chillies for about 7 minutes until blackened in spots. Turn them over and continue to blacken for about another 7 minutes. Remove from the heat and set aside to cool at room temperature. Once they are cool enough to handle, peel the tomatoes and discard the skins. Stem the chillies and peel and discard the skin.

Remove the stems from the guajillo and chipotle chillies and tear them open. Shake out and discard the seeds. Remove and discard the veins.

Set a large cast-iron pan over medium heat for 5 minutes. Add the oregano and cumin seeds and toast briefly for 15 seconds, shaking the pan, until fragrant. Remove from the heat, transfer to a spice mill or coffee grinder and grind to a fine powder.

Reheat the cast-iron pan over medium heat. Toast the guajillo and chipotle chillies, turning them from time to time until the pan smokes, about 45 seconds.

Remove the pan from the heat and transfer the chillies to a bowl. Cover them with hot tap water and place a heavy plate over the chillies to keep them submerged. Set aside to soak for 30 minutes.

Add the garlic cloves to the pan and roast, turning them from time to time until softened slightly and blackened in spots, about 6 minutes. Turn off the heat, remove the garlic from the pan, and set aside to cool at room temperature. Once they are cool enough to handle, peel the garlic cloves and discard the skins.

Drain the soaked chillies and discard the liquid. Place them in a blender along with the ground spices and roasted garlic, the salt, sugar, vinegar, lemon juice and 60 ml (¼ cup) water. Purée on high speed until completely smooth, working in batches if necessary.

Set up a medium-mesh sieve over a bowl and pass the purée through the strainer. Transfer to a container or refrigerate until ready to use. The salsa will keep for up to 3 days.

PICCALILLI

MAKES 1 KG (2 LB 4 OZ)

INGREDIENTS

250 g (9 oz) zucchini (courgettes)
  or cucumbers
300 g (10½ oz) cauliflower florets
150 g (5½ oz) green beans, trimmed
  and cut into short lengths
250 g (9 oz) French shallots or small
  pickling onions, quartered
75 g (generous ½ cup) sea salt
4 tbsp cornflour
75 g (⅓ cup) sugar
1 tbsp mustard powder
1 tsp ground turmeric
1 tsp ground ginger
500 ml (2 cups) malt vinegar

METHOD

Cut the zucchini into half or quarters
lengthways, then slice thickly. If using a
cucumber, cut in half lengthways, scoop
out and discard the seeds, then cut in half
again and slice.

Layer the vegetables in a bowl, sprinkling
with the salt as you layer them. Toss
together to coat with the salt. Cover and
allow to stand for 24 hours.

Drain the vegetables and rinse very well in
cold water. Drain again and allow to dry in
a colander on a tea towel.

Mix the cornflour, sugar, mustard powder,
turmeric and ginger together in a pan over
low heat with a little of the vinegar to form
a smooth paste. Make sure that you get the
mixture lump free at this stage.

Gradually stir in the remaining vinegar.
Cook over low heat, stirring for about
10 minutes until the mixture comes to the
boil and thickens.

Add the vegetables and cook gently for
2–3 minutes. Spoon into hot sterilised jars
and seal. Piccalilli will keep for 6 months
in a cool, dark place.

FRIED GARLIC

MAKES 85 G (3 OZ)

INGREDIENTS

About 500 ml (2 cups) vegetable oil
175 g (6 oz) garlic cloves, cut into
  3 mm (⅛ inch) slices

EQUIPMENT

Cooking thermometer

METHOD

Set a sieve over a heatproof container.
Pour enough oil into a small saucepan
to reach a depth of 2 cm (¾ inch). Set
the pan over high heat and bring the oil
to 135°C (275°F). Add the garlic, then
immediately turn the heat to low and
stir once or twice.

Cook, stirring and scraping the sides
occasionally and adjusting the heat
to maintain a steady sizzle, for about
4–5 minutes until the garlic is light
golden brown and crisp. If the process
takes less time, that means the oil is
too hot and you risk a bitter result.
You'll get the hang of it.

Pour the pan's contents through the
sieve set over the container, reserving
the oil. Gently shake the sieve, then
drain and cool in one layer on paper
towel. Because the garlic continues to
cook after leaving the oil, it will have
gone from light to golden brown.

The fried garlic will keep in an airtight
container in a cool, dry place (not in
the fridge) for up to 2 days. Any more
and you risk losing crunch and flavour.
The strained oil keeps in an airtight
container for up to 2 weeks.

07

SERIOUSLY

WHIPPED

Dessert

THIS IS A COLLECTION OF SOME OF MY FAVOURITE
DESSERTS, WHICH ARE A GREAT WAY TO OVERINDULGE AFTER
A HECTIC MEAL. DESSERT IS ALSO THE PART OF THE MEAL MY
KIDS REALLY LOOK FORWARD TO, HENCE MY ADDING HEAPS
OF BOOZE TO MOST OF THE RECIPES SO YOU GET THE
SATISFACTION OF TELLING THEM THAT THEY CAN'T HAVE ANY,
LEAVING MORE FOR YOU. QUICK MATH.

BLACK FOREST CAKE

MAKES 1 CAKE

This is my favourite cake and one I always request for my birthday. It's heavy on the Kirsch, but that's only because I have no self control and love Kirsch. Don't substitute anything for anything in this recipe. Take the plunge and thank me later.

INGREDIENTS

175 g (scant ¾ cup) unsalted butter, plus extra for greasing
75 g (2½ oz) good-quality dark chocolate, broken into chunks
300 g (2 cups) plain flour
375 g (1⅔ cups) caster sugar
25 g (¼ cup) cocoa powder
1 tsp bicarbonate of soda (baking soda)
Pinch of sea salt flakes
2 medium eggs
200 ml (generous ¾ cup) buttermilk

TO ASSEMBLE

425 g (15 oz) cherries soaked in Kirsch
100 g (3½ oz) black cherry jam
500 ml (2 cups) thick (double) cream
125 g (4½ oz) good-quality dark chocolate, chopped
3 tbsp icing (confectioners') sugar
50 g (½ cup) cocoa powder
1 punnet of fresh cherries
Chocolate shards (optional)

METHOD

Preheat the oven to 180°C (350°F). Grease and line the base of three 20 cm (8 inch) cake tins. Boil the kettle.

Put the butter and chocolate in a small saucepan and gently heat, stirring, until completely melted.

Mix together the flour, sugar, cocoa, bicarbonate of soda and sea salt in a mixing bowl. Whisk the eggs and buttermilk together. Scrape the melted chocolate mixture and egg mixture into the dry ingredients, add 100 ml (scant ½ cup) boiling water and whizz briefly with an electric whisk until the cake batter is lump free.

Divide the mixture among the tins and bake for 25 minutes, swapping the tins round after 20 mins if they're on different shelves. To test they're done, push in a skewer and check that it comes out clean.

Prick the cakes a few times with a skewer. Drain the cherries, reserving 200 ml (generous ¾ cup) of the Kirsch and drizzling that over the cakes. Cool the cakes. Mix together the cherries and jam.

To make the icing, tip 200 ml (generous ¾ cup) of the cream into a pan and heat until just below simmering point. Put the chocolate in a heatproof bowl, pour over the hot cream and stir until melted. Set aside until spreadable.

When the cakes are cool, whisk the remaining cream, icing sugar and cocoa together until softly whipped and the cocoa powder is dissolved. Spread over two of the cakes and sandwich the three cakes together. Mask the sides with the icing until they are vaguely neat (get your plasterer mate to pop over and help you).

Pipe 12 florets of icing around the top of the cake with a fresh cherry on top of each weirdo turret (serve any remaining cherries on the side). Spoon the rest of the jammy cherries into the centre of the cake and if you are very lavish, throw down some chocolate shards on the top and then enter the cake in the GREAT BRITISH BAKE OFF!

206

PEACH MELBA

SERVES 4

'Adelaide, that city of the 3 P's –
Parsons, pubs and prostitutes.'
— Dame Nellie Melba, 1861–1931

N&M (her street name) is considered one of the greatest singers of all time and she bloody owned the penthouse above Africola! How's that for a coincidence? Not only do we occasionally cook for the clergy, the building was a pub and we have been described as a brothel. This is my version of the classic dessert that was created in her honour.

INGREDIENTS

4 ripe peaches
4 tbsp sugar
2 tbsp flaked almonds
500 g (1 lb 2 oz) raspberries
3 tbsp icing (confectioners') sugar
2 tsp raspberry vinegar
4 scoops of good vanilla ice-cream

METHOD

Blanch the peaches in a pan of boiling water for a minute, then lift them out with a slotted spoon and refresh in iced water. Once they're cool enough to handle, slip off their skins, cut in half and discard the stones.

Put the peach halves in a shallow dish, sprinkle over the sugar, then set aside for about an hour to macerate, preferably in the fridge, turning a couple of times.

Meanwhile, toast the almonds in a hot oven until lightly golden and leave to cool.

Blitz two-thirds of the raspberries with the icing sugar and the raspberry vinegar, then adjust to taste and push through a fine sieve to make a smooth sauce. Stir in the remaining raspberries and put in the fridge until you're ready to eat.

To serve, put two peach halves in each dish and add a scoop of vanilla ice-cream. Pour the sauce over the top and finish with a sprinkling of flaked almonds.

CHOC ORANGE TORTE

MAKES 1 TORTE

We bake this recipe in our wood oven and on the finish, throw orange rind and rosemary on the fire and close the oven door for an aromatic smoked finish. If you don't have a wood oven, use a domestic one and then sage smudge the kitchen to get rid of any bad spirits that may be lurking around. It won't affect the flavour of the torte, but your chakras will be cleansed enough to eat the whole batch guilt-free.

CHOCOLATE FILLING

300 g (10½ oz) good-quality dark chocolate
300 ml (1¼ cups) thick (double) cream
135 ml (½ cup) milk
70 g (scant ¼ cup) honey
Zest of 1 orange
Healthy splash of Cointreau
3 eggs
Grated orange zest, to garnish

CHOCOLATE SHORTCRUST BASE

125 g (generous ¾ cup) plain flour
125 g (½ cup) butter, cubed, plus extra for greasing
1 tbsp sea salt
25 g (scant ¼ cup) sugar
25 g (¼ cup) cocoa powder
1 egg

EQUIPMENT

Wood oven, rosemary sprigs and 10 orange rinds (optional)

METHOD

Preheat the oven to 180°C (350°F). Grease and line a large, deep baking tray.

Melt all the ingredients for the chocolate filling (except the eggs) together over low heat. Take off the heat and let the mixture cool.

Whisk in the eggs slowly until the mix becomes thick and glossy like a ganache. Set aside.

To make the base, beat the flour, butter, salt and sugar together.

Add the cocoa and the egg and mix until the dough comes together. Let the base rest for 20 minutes, then roll the dough out for your base on a lightly floured surface.

Fill the prepared baking tray with the base and blind bake for 12 minutes or until it starts to just colour.

When the base has cooled a little, add the choc filling so it is about 5 cm (2 inches) high.

Bake in the wood oven, then use the smoking technique spoken about in the intro to bake the torte at 160°C (315°F) for 20 minutes. Alternatively, bake in a normal oven at the same temperature, but the smudging is optional. Slice into bars to serve and garnish with orange zest.

CHOCOLATE AND EUCALYPTUS BARS

MAKES 1 BAR

This recipe was inspired by all the bloody gum trees we have in Australia. Mint and chocolate work and mint and eucalyptus taste similar, so pairing eucalyptus and chocolate is a no-brainer.

INGREDIENTS

220 g (8 oz) shortbread biscuits
4 tbsp melted unsalted butter, cooled
Cocoa powder, to dust

SPEARMINT CARAMEL

100 ml (scant ½ cup) single (pure) cream
3 drops of peppermint essence
12 eucalyptus leaves or large mint leaves
110 g (½ cup) caster sugar
3 tbsp unsalted butter

MINT GANACHE

200 ml (generous ¾ cup) thick (double) cream
5 eucalyptus leaves or large mint leaves
2 tbsp unsalted butter, chopped
2 tbsp glucose syrup
3 drops of peppermint essence
200 g (8 oz) good-quality dark chocolate, chopped

MILK CHOCOLATE GLAZE

250 g (9 oz) good-quality milk chocolate, chopped
2 tbsp sunflower oil

METHOD

Grease a 1-litre (4-cup) terrine mould and line the base with baking parchment.

Whizz the shortbread in a food processor to crumbs. Add the butter and whizz again to combine. Press evenly into the base of the mould.

For the spearmint caramel, place the cream, peppermint essence and eucalyptus or mint in a saucepan over medium–low heat. Bring to the boil, then remove from the heat and set aside for 20 minutes to infuse. Strain, discarding the leaves.

Melt the sugar in a frying pan over medium–high heat, swirling the pan for 5 minutes or until a golden caramel forms. Add the butter and swirl the pan, then add the infused cream, swirling to combine. Remove from the heat and pour evenly over the shortbread base. Set aside for 30 minutes to firm up slightly.

For the mint ganache, place all the ingredients, except the chocolate, in a saucepan over medium heat and bring to just below boiling point. Remove from the heat. Set aside for 20 minutes to infuse.

Remove the leaves and discard. Return the pan to medium heat and bring to a simmer.

Place the chocolate in a heatproof bowl and pour over the cream mixture, stirring until melted and smooth. Pour this over the caramel layer. Cover and chill for 4 hours or until set.

For the milk chocolate glaze, place the chocolate and oil in a heatproof bowl set over a pan of simmering water (don't let the bowl touch the water), stirring until melted and smooth. Set aside to cool.

Carefully turn out the bar onto a well-oiled rack set over a tray, so that the biscuit base sits on the rack and the ganache layer is facing up. Pour the melted chocolate over the top and sides, smoothing with a palette knife. Chill for 15 minutes to set.

Dust the bar with cocoa, then, using a hot sharp knife, cut into slices to serve.

MILK TART

★ ★ ★

MAKES 1 TART

This dish is a South African staple, served mainly on a Sunday, after church with your extended family. The taste of this tart is rich, but with a light mouthfeel. It's a dessert to wear pants for.

SWEET PASTRY

Butter or oil spray, for greasing
225 g (1½ cups) plain flour
¼ tsp fine sea salt
40 g (⅓ cup) icing (confectioners') sugar
125 g (½ cup) chilled unsalted butter,
    cut into small pieces
1 large egg yolk

MILK FILLING

2 tbsp butter
½ tsp ground nutmeg
560 ml (2¼ cups) milk
2 tbsp plain flour
2 tbsp cornflour
110 g (½ cup) sugar
½ tbsp vanilla extract
½ tbsp almond essence
2 eggs
½ tsp ground cinnamon

METHOD

Butter or spray a 23 cm (9 inch) tart tin with a removable bottom – making sure it is adequately coated.

To make the pastry, place the flour, salt and sugar in a food processor and pulse a couple of times to mix the ingredients. Throw in the butter and pulse until a rough dough forms.

Add the egg yolk, pulsing until the dough starts to stiffen. Remove the dough and place on a work surface. Knead just enough to incorporate all the dough, working the dough as little as possible. Do not overwork the dough; otherwise it'll be too tough.

When the dough is ready, it will be barely moistened and come together into a ball.

Lightly press the dough into the prepared tart tin, working from the centre up until the bottom and sides are fully covered with pastry. Again, be very gentle when pressing the dough into the tart tin.

Place the tart tin in the freezer and freeze for at least 30 minutes or more. This helps prevent the dough from rising.

Preheat the oven to 200°C (400°F). Place baking beans into the pastry case and blind bake the crust for about 20–25 minutes or until the crust is dry and golden brown. Set aside.

To make the milk filling, place a saucepan over medium heat and add the butter, nutmeg and milk. Bring to the boil and then remove from the heat.

In another bowl, mix together the flour, cornflour, sugar, vanilla and almond essence, then whisk in the eggs until smooth. Pour into the saucepan and gently whisk, making sure there are no lumps.

Now return the pan back to the heat and keep stirring constantly until the mixture starts to bubble. Cook for about 5–6 minutes after it starts bubbling.

Remove the pan from the heat and pour the mixture into the baked pastry shell. Sprinkle with cinnamon. Chill until ready to be served.

Or if this recipe is way too difficult, I suggest my mum's version:

1 bottle of vodka
250 ml (1 cup) condensed milk
Sprinkle of ground cinnamon

Pour the vodka into a bowl, add the condensed milk and whisk until emulsified. Using a funnel, pour the liquids back into the bottle.

Serve in chilled shot glasses and finish with a little sprinkle of cinnamon. Give to your gran.

213

CH 07: SERIOUSLY WHIPPED DESSERT

ETON MESS

MAKES 1 BIG BOWL/6 JARS

This is a spicy addition to the Eton mess catalogue.

INGREDIENTS

500 g (1 lb 2 oz) rhubarb
½ pomegranate
100 g (scant ½ cup) caster sugar
2 tsp rose water
5 vanilla pods
1 litre (4 cups) thick (double) cream
250 ml (1 cup) crème fraîche
100 g (scant 1 cup) icing (confectioners')
   sugar, sieved
1 punnet of raspberries, to garnish (optional)

MERINGUES

500 g (1 lb 2 oz) egg whites
Pinch of salt
500 g (2¼ cups) caster sugar
500 g (4 cups) icing (confectioners') sugar
75 g (generous ½ cup) cornflour
75 g (2½ oz) dried rose petals,
   plus more to garnish
50 g (2 oz) Sichuan pepper

METHOD

Top and tail your rhubarb and cut into 10 cm (4 inch) length pieces. Place in a saucepan with the pomegranate seeds and cover with the caster sugar, 300 ml (1¼ cups) water, rose water and 2 vanilla pods. Place over heat and gently simmer until the rhubarb is just soft. Remove from the heat and set aside to cool.

Preheat the oven to 120°C (235°F). Line two baking trays with baking parchment.

To make the meringues, whisk the egg whites and pinch of salt in a mixer for 3–4 minutes until firm peaks form. With the motor running, gradually add the caster sugar and whisk for 2–3 minutes until thick and glossy.

Sieve the icing sugar and cornflour over and gently fold in to combine. Sprinkle in the dried rose petals and Sichuan pepper and mix in, then spoon 8 cm (3¼ inch) diameter mounds onto the baking trays.

Bake the meringues for 45–50 minutes, until they lift easily from the trays and are crisp but not coloured. Turn off the heat and leave the meringues to cool completely inside the oven.

Whisk the thick cream, crème fraîche and icing sugar together in a separate large bowl until soft peaks form. Split the remaining vanilla pods in half and scrape the seeds from the pods into the mixture.

Scatter half the rhubarb into the base of a serving bowl or six jars, spread with half the cream mixture, and coarsely crumble half the meringue over the top. Repeat with the remaining ingredients and decorate with rose petals.

VETKOEK WITH ROASTED QUINCES AND MATURE CHEDDAR

MAKES 12–16 SMALL VETKOEK

Deep-fried, these little bad boys are the South African version of the doughnut and are perfect for sweet and savoury fillings. Traditionally they are served with curried mince, which is excellent, but may also cause diabetes. When weapon chef Luke Burgess cooked at Africola, the crazy fool served them with porcini ice cream and porcini powder, which was super weird but super delicious – just like Luke.

INGREDIENTS

150 g (5½ oz) strong mature cheddar

VETKOEK

360 g (2⅓ cups) plain flour
1 x 10 g (¼ oz) sachet of active dry yeast
1 tsp salt
1 tbsp sugar
185 ml (¾ cup) lukewarm water
Canola oil, for frying

ROASTED QUINCE

4 heaped tbsp sugar
4 whole cloves
10 coriander seeds
10 fennel seeds
2 star anise
4 smallish quinces
½ lemon
200 ml (generous ¾ cup) maple syrup

METHOD

To make the vetkoek, combine the dry ingredients in a large bowl. Add the water a little at a time, mixing with a wooden spoon until a wet dough forms.

Knead the dough in the bowl for 5 minutes, until it springs back if you press it with your finger. Cover the bowl with plastic wrap and allow the dough to rise for 30–45 minutes or until doubled in size.

To make the roasted quinces, add the sugar and 500 ml (2 cups) water to a saucepan and bring to the boil. Add the cloves, coriander seeds, fennel seeds and star anise. Peel and halve the quinces and rub them with lemon to stop them browning.

Lower the quinces into the sugar syrup and let them simmer till tender. They may be ready in 25 minutes or perhaps take a little longer, depending on their size and ripeness.

Preheat the oven to 180°C (350°F). When the quinces are tender to the point of a knife, lift them out and put them in a shallow baking dish or roasting tin. Take 150 ml (generous ½ cup) of the cooking liquid along with the aromatics, add the maple syrup and pour over the quinces. Bake for 30 minutes or until very soft and tender.

Meanwhile, heat the canola oil in a saucepan over medium heat. Knock the risen dough back and divide into 12–16 equal-sized vetkoek. Gently drop 4 vetkoek into the oil and cover the saucepan with a lid (this allows them to partially steam while frying).

Cook for 2 minutes, or until golden on one side, then turn and cook the other side. When cooked through and golden, remove the vetkoek from the oil and drain on paper towel.

Once the quinces have cooled, slice them and stuff into the vetkoek, making sure to spoon some of the juices inside. Microplane or finely grate the cheddar over the top.

WEIRDO CARAMEL CUSTARD

SERVES 4

This is a crème caramel, but is actually a lot more stable with a richer finish due to the evaporated milk.

INGREDIENTS

300 ml (1¼ cups) evaporated milk
100 g (scant ½ cup) sugar
1 vanilla pod
300 ml (1¼ cups) thick (double) cream
150 g (5½ oz) egg yolks

CARAMEL

100 g (scant ½ cup) sugar
3 cardamom pods
2 star anise

EQUIPMENT

Custard cups
Bain marie

METHOD

Place the closed tin of evaporated milk into a small saucepan of boiling water. Boil for 2 hours, then set aside to cool.

Place the sugar in a medium bowl. Split the vanilla pod in half and scrape the seeds from the vanilla pod into the sugar. Reserve the pod for another use. Use your fingers to rub the seeds and the sugar together, breaking up the vanilla seeds until they are evenly dispersed in the sugar.

Add the evaporated milk, cream and egg yolks to the bowl and whisk until evenly combined, adding as little air as possible.

Strain the custard through a fine mesh strainer and let it rest for 30 minutes, allowing any foamy air bubbles to rise to the top and be spooned off.

To make the caramel, first set 4 custard cups near the stove. Place the sugar and 75 ml (⅓ cup) water in a small saucepan and place over medium heat, stirring very gently just until the sugar is moist. Once the syrup starts to boil, add the cardamom and star anise, washing any stray sugar crystals that form on the sides of the pan with a moist brush. Continue to cook until the sugar reaches a golden caramel. Check the colour of your caramel by dipping a piece of white paper in the caramel – it will always look darker in the pan than it really is. Cook until the colour is a tawny, golden brown, like the colour of a newborn fawn.

Working quickly, remove the pan from the heat and divide the caramel into the custard cups. Swirl the hot caramel around the cups if necessary to ensure it coats the bottoms evenly.

Let the caramel cool completely in the cups, then divide the prepared custard into the cups. Cover each cup individually with foil.

Steam in a bain marie for 12–15 minutes or until cooked. They should be firm and wobbly.

BOOZYMISU

MAKES 1 LARGE BOWL

I've kept this recipe as easy and as quick as possible, but made sure I added heaps more booze than I normally would. The addition of tequila is a nice contrast and really brings out the chocolate.

INGREDIENTS

600 ml (2½ cups) thick (double) cream
300 g (1¼ cups) mascarpone
75 ml (⅓ cup) Marsala
2½ tbsp tequila
2½ tbsp Frangelico
5 tbsp caster sugar
300 ml (1¼ cups) strong coffee, made with
   4 tbsp coffee granules and
   300 ml (1¼ cups) boiling water
1 pack of sponge fingers
100 g (3½ oz) good-quality dark chocolate
2 tsp cocoa powder

METHOD

Put the cream, mascarpone, all the booze and the caster sugar in a large bowl. Whisk until the cream and mascarpone have completely combined and have the consistency of thickly whipped cream.

Pour the coffee into a shallow dish. Dip in a few of the sponge fingers at a time, turning for a few seconds until they are nicely soaked, but not soggy. Layer these into your bowl until you have used half the sponge fingers, then spread over half of the creamy mixture.

Using the coarse side of the grater, grate over some of the dark chocolate, then repeat the layers (you should use up all the coffee), finishing with the creamy layer.

Cover and chill for a few hours or overnight. The tiramisu can now be kept in the fridge for up to 2 days. To serve, dust with cocoa powder and grate over the remainder of the chocolate.

WOLF CREEK

Bakery Counter

DESSERTS

THESE RECIPES ARE A COLLECTION OF WHAT YOU WOULD
USUALLY FIND IN BAKERIES IN REGIONAL AUSTRALIA. PACKED
WITH SUGAR AND PRETTY FILLING TO BOOT, A PERFECT SNACK
WHILE ESCAPING FROM A SERIAL KILLER.

SNOT BLOCKS AKA VANILLA SLICE

MAKES 12 SLICES

ROUGH PUFF PASTRY

225 g (1½ cups) plain flour
1 tsp sea salt
200 g (generous ¾ cup) chilled unsalted butter,
    cut into 1 cm (½ inch) cubes

CRÈME PÂTISSIÈRE

500 ml (2 cups) milk
2 vanilla pods
100 g (scant ½ cup) caster sugar
4 egg yolks
40 g (⅓ cup) cornflour
50 g (scant ¼ cup) unsalted butter

ICING

200 g (1⅔ cups) icing (confectioners') sugar
80 g (3 oz) good-quality dark chocolate, melted

EQUIPMENT

Piping bag fitted with a small plain nozzle
Toothpicks

METHOD

In a large bowl, mix the flour and salt together. Rub in a third of the butter until the mixture resembles fine breadcrumbs, then roughly rub in the remaining butter, leaving large lumps. Add 140–160 ml (generous ½ cup) water a little at a time until the pastry just binds together (you may not need all the water).

Tip the pastry out onto a floured work surface. Roll into a narrow rectangle about 2.5 cm (1 inch) thick.

With the pastry vertically in front of you, fold the bottom third of the pastry up onto the middle third, then the top third down onto the other thirds. This is called a turn. Wrap the pastry in plastic wrap and place in the fridge to chill for 10 minutes.

Take out of the fridge and, with a rolling pin, roll out again into a narrow rectangle, then repeat the turn as before.

Chill again and repeat the rolling and turning once more, so a total of three times. Wrap the pastry in plastic wrap and return to the fridge to rest.

While the pastry is resting, make the crème pâtissière. Pour the milk into a saucepan. Split the vanilla pods in half and scrape the seeds into the milk along with the split pods. Bring the milk mixture to the boil, then remove from the heat.

Whisk the sugar, egg yolks and cornflour together in a large bowl.

Pour a little of the hot milk onto the egg mixture, whisking continuously. Whisk in the rest of the hot milk until well combined, then return to the pan. Cook the mixture over a gentle heat, stirring continuously, until the mixture becomes thick. It will just come to the boil.

Remove from the heat and pass the mixture through a sieve into a clean bowl. Add the butter and stir until melted and thoroughly combined. Leave to cool, cover with plastic wrap and then chill well before using.

Preheat the oven to 220°C (425°F). Line two baking trays with baking parchment.

Divide the pastry into two equal pieces and roll out both pieces to a 20 cm (8 inch) square, 5 mm (¼ inch) thick. Place each pastry sheet on the lined baking trays and chill for 10–15 minutes.

Bake the pastry sheets for 10–15 minutes or until golden brown and crisp. Set aside to cool.

While the pastry bakes, line a deep 23 cm (9 inch) square baking tray with foil, with plenty of extra foil at the sides (the extra foil allows you to lift out the assembled slices).

Place one pastry sheet in the bottom of the lined baking tray (reserve the prettiest piece for the top). Spread the crème pâtissière evenly onto the pastry in the baking tray before placing the other piece of pastry on top. Refrigerate while making the icing.

For the icing, sift the icing sugar into a bowl. Stir in 5 teaspoons of cold water until combined and then set aside.

Transfer the melted chocolate into a piping bag fitted with a small plain nozzle and set aside to firm up slightly.

Take the custard slice from the fridge and spread the icing over the top layer of pastry. Using the piping bag, draw ten parallel lines along the top of the icing in one direction. Using a toothpick, pull the parallel lines about 2.5 cm (1 inch) across the melted chocolate and icing in alternating directions to create a feathered effect. Place the slice back into the fridge to set.

Cut the finished vanilla slice into pieces. Using the foil, carefully lift the portioned vanilla slices out of the tray and place on a serving platter.

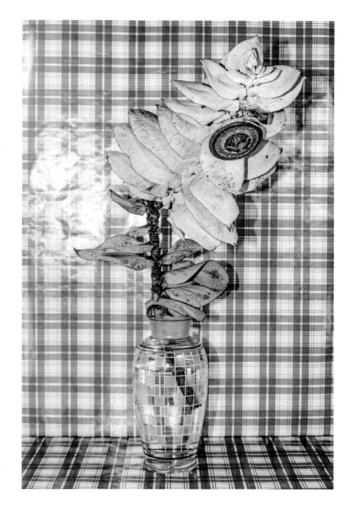

PORTUGUESE CUSTARD TARTS (PASTÉIS DE NATA)

MAKES 24 TARTS

DOUGH

275 g (generous 1¾ cups) plain flour
¼ tsp sea salt
205 ml (generous ¾ cup) fridge-cold water
225 g (scant 1 cup) room-temperature unsalted
  butter, stirred until smooth

CUSTARD

3 tbsp plain flour
300 ml (1¼ cups) milk
265 g (scant 1¼ cups) sugar
1 cinnamon stick
½ tsp vanilla extract
6 large egg yolks, whisked

GARNISH

Icing (confectioners') sugar
Ground cinnamon

EQUIPMENT

Pastry scraper
Cooking thermometer
2 non-stick 12-cup mini muffin tins
  (5 x 1.5 cm/2 x ⅝ inch size)

METHOD

To make the dough, in a stand mixer fitted with a dough hook, mix together the flour, salt and cold water for about 30 seconds until a soft, pillowy dough forms that pulls away from the sides of the bowl.

Generously flour a work surface and pat the dough into a 15 cm (6 inch) square using a pastry scraper. Flour the dough, cover with plastic wrap, and let it rest at room temperature for 15 minutes.

Roll the dough into a 46 cm (18 inch) square. As you work, use the scraper to lift the dough to make sure the underside isn't sticking to your work surface.

Brush the excess flour off the top of the dough, trim any uneven edges and, using a small offset spatula, dot and then spread the left two-thirds portion of the dough with a little less than a third of the butter, being careful to leave a 2.5 cm (1 inch) plain border around the edge of the dough.

Neatly fold the unbuttered right third of the dough (using the pastry scraper to loosen it if it sticks) over the rest of the dough. Brush off any excess flour, then fold over the left third of the dough. Starting from the top, pat down the dough with your hand to release any air bubbles, and then pinch the edges of the dough to seal. Brush off any excess flour.

Turn the dough 90° to the left so the fold is facing you. Lift the dough and flour the work surface. Once again, roll it out to a 46 cm (18 inch) square, then dot the left two-thirds of the dough with a third of the butter and smear it over the dough. Fold the dough as directed in the previous steps.

For the last rolling, turn the dough 90° to the left and roll out the dough to a 53 x 46 cm (21 x 18 inch) rectangle, with the shorter side facing you. Spread the remaining butter over the entire surface of the dough.

Using the spatula as an aid, lift the edge of dough closest to you and roll the dough away from you into a tight log, brushing the excess flour from the underside as you go. Trim the ends and cut the log in half. Wrap each piece in plastic wrap and chill for 2 hours or preferably overnight (the pastry can be frozen for up to 3 months).

To make the custard, in a medium bowl whisk the flour and 60 ml (¼ cup) of the milk until smooth.

Bring the sugar, cinnamon and 160 ml (generous ½ cup) water to the boil in a small saucepan and cook until a cooking thermometer registers 100°C (212°F). Do not stir.

Meanwhile, in another small saucepan, scald the remaining milk. Whisk the hot milk into the flour mixture.

Remove the cinnamon stick and then pour the sugar syrup in a thin stream into the hot milk-and-flour mixture, whisking briskly. Add the vanilla and stir for a minute until very warm but not hot. Whisk in the yolks, strain the mixture into a bowl, cover with plastic wrap and set aside. The custard will be thin – that is as it should be (you can refrigerate the custard for up to 3 days).

To assemble and bake the pastries, place an oven rack in the top third position and preheat the oven to 220°C (425°F). Remove the pastry logs from the fridge and roll them back and forth on a lightly floured surface until they are about 2.5 cm (1 inch) in diameter and 40 cm (16 inches) long. Cut them into 1.5 cm (⅝ inch) pieces.

Place one piece of pastry dough, cut-side down, in each well of the 12-cup mini muffin tins. Allow the dough pieces to soften for several minutes until pliable.

Have a small cup of water nearby. Dip your thumbs in the water, then straight down into the middle of each dough spiral. Flatten it against the bottom of the cup to a thickness of about 2 mm (less than ⅛ inch), then smooth the dough up the sides and create a raised lip about 3 mm (⅛ inch) above each tin. The pastry bottoms should be thinner than the tops.

Fill each cup three-quarters full with the cool custard. Bake the pastries until the edges of the dough are cooked and brown – about 8–9 minutes.

Remove from the oven and allow the pastéis to cool for a few minutes in the tins, then transfer to a wire rack and cool until just warm. Sprinkle the pastéis generously with icing sugar, then cinnamon, and serve. These are best consumed the same day they're made.

NEENISH TARTS

MAKES 12 TARTS

Basically the half-and-half iced tooth killer. There is pastry, cake, mock cream, jam, so much icing. It basically has too much of everything. It's as unforgettable as diabetes. This recipe has been taken from one of the Country Women's Association's baking pamphlets. They are a true force of good and without them our rural farming communities would struggle to maintain their good spirits in the face of the crippling droughts that devastate our landscape.

PASTRY

130 g (scant 1 cup) plain flour
80 g (⅓ cup) chilled unsalted butter, cubed
2 tbsp sugar
Pinch of salt
1 egg yolk
1½ tbsp iced water
165 g (½ cup) strawberry jam

CREAM

1 tbsp boiling water
½ tsp gelatine powder
30 g (¼ cup) icing (confectioners') sugar
2 tbsp milk
115 g (scant ½ cup) softened unsalted butter
1 tsp vanilla extract

ICING

125 g (1 cup) icing (confectioners') sugar, sifted
3 tsp milk
2 tsp cocoa powder
Pink food colouring

EQUIPMENT

Large round cookie cutter
  (approx. 8.5–9 cm / 3½ inches)

METHOD

To make the pastry, pulse the flour, butter, sugar and salt in a food processor until it looks like wet sand. Add the egg yolk and pulse until mixed. Add the water, ½ tablespoon at a time, and pulse between each addition until the dough starts clumping together.

Turn the dough out on a lightly floured surface and knead just until smooth. Press into a disc, wrap in plastic wrap and refrigerate for at least half an hour.

Preheat the oven to 200°C (400°F). Grease and lightly flour a 12-hole muffin tin.

Roll the dough out to 2 mm (less than ⅛ inch) thick and use a large round cookie cutter to cut out rounds of pastry. Gently drop them down into each hole of the muffin tin, making sure they're level. The pastry should come about 2 cm (¾ inch) up the side of the holes. Return to the fridge for 15 minutes.

Prick the base of each case with a fork and bake for 10–12 minutes until starting to turn golden. Transfer to a wire rack until completely cool. Spread 1–2 teaspoons of jam over the base of each case.

To make the cream, tip the boiling water into a small dish and sprinkle the gelatine over the top. Mix with a fork, then allow to sit for 5 minutes.

Add the sugar and milk to a saucepan and heat over a very low heat until the sugar dissolves. Give the gelatine another stir, then pour it into the hot milk and stir until completely dissolved. Let the mixture cool to room temperature before continuing.

Beat the butter and vanilla until light and creamy. Slowly pour in the milk mixture, constantly beating.

Spread the cream over the tarts and use a spatula to make the tops level.

To make the icing, mix the icing sugar and the milk together until you have a smooth, spreadable consistency. Transfer half to a separate bowl, add the cocoa and mix well. Add just a small amount of pink food colouring to the other half and mix.

Use a spatula to spread pink icing over half of each tart, then allow to set for 10–15 minutes at room temperature. Repeat with the chocolate icing. Serve.

GRILLED COCONUT RICE AND BANANA PASTE

SERVES 4

One of the simplest and most delicious desserts out there – incredibly moreish and satisfying.

INGREDIENTS

4 banana leaves, at room temperature
1 banana, sliced lengthways

STICKY RICE

220 g (8 oz) white sticky rice, washed to remove excess starch (be careful not to break the grains), soaked overnight in 500 ml (2 cups) water
4 pandan leaves
250 ml (1 cup) thick, full-fat coconut cream
165 g (¾ cup) caster sugar
2 tsp sea salt flakes

BANANA PASTE

80 ml (⅓ cup) coconut cream
60 g (⅓ cup) light palm sugar (jaggery), crushed
Small pinch of salt
2 small very ripe bananas, puréed to give 20 g (4¼ oz) purée
Pinch of ground cloves
1½ tbsp young coconut water

EQUIPMENT

Steamer
Charcoal barbecue or chargrill pan
Toothpicks

METHOD

For the sticky rice, rinse and drain the rice, then place in a steamer lined with a damp tea towel, with the rice slightly piled up in the centre. Put the steamer over a pan of boiling water. Add two pandan leaves to the water to perfume the steam, then steam the rice, covered, topping up boiling water as necessary, for 20–25 minutes until the rice is just tender (test grains from the centre for doneness).

Meanwhile, stir the coconut cream, sugar, sea salt flakes and the remaining pandan leaves in a bowl for 2–3 minutes until the sugar dissolves.

When the rice is cooked, turn off the heat and add the rice to the coconut cream mixture. Stir to combine, then return to the steamer, cover and stand over hot water over a very low heat for 2–3 hours until the rice absorbs the liquid and just about holds its own shape.

For the banana paste, simmer the coconut cream in a pan over medium heat for 2–3 minutes until beginning to separate. Add the palm sugar and salt and stir for 30 seconds–1 minute to dissolve. Stir in the banana purée and cloves, then gradually add the coconut water and gently stir over low–medium heat for 12–15 minutes until the paste pulls away from the sides of the wok. Set aside to cool.

Light a barbecue and burn down to embers or heat a chargrill pan. Heat the banana leaves for 10–20 seconds over the flame or in the pan until soft and glossy. Trim the hard edges and discard the yellow parts, then cut two leaves into six 20 x 25 cm (8 x 10 inch) pieces, and the other two into six 14 x 20 cm (5½ x 8 inch) pieces. Wipe on both sides with a clean, damp cloth, then place the large pieces shiny-side down on a work surface. Now place the small pieces shiny-side up on top of them and spoon 2 heaped tablespoonfuls of rice onto the small leaf pieces. Spoon over 2 teaspoons of banana paste, top with banana slivers and spoon another tablespoonful of rice on top. Fold the edges of the leaves inwards to enclose, and secure the parcels with toothpicks. Grill, turning once, over low heat for 15–20 minutes until fragrant and toasty with chargrill marks on the outside. Serve warm.

FINGER BANG BUNS

MAKES 20 BUNS

A South Australian classic! Basically a submarine-shaped hot cross bun with heaps of icing.

INGREDIENTS

500 g (1 lb 2 oz) white bread mix
100 g (scant ½ cup) caster sugar
1 egg
250–300 ml (1–1¼ cups) lukewarm water
Oil, for greasing
350 g (2¾ cups) icing (confectioners') sugar
Food colouring (optional)
Sprinkles

METHOD

Pulse together the bread mix and sugar in a food processor or stand mixer. While the motor is running, add the egg and the lukewarm water until a soft dough is formed.

Knead the dough on a lightly floured surface for about 5–10 minutes until smooth. Add to an oiled bowl, cover with oiled plastic wrap, and leave in a warm place until doubled in size – about 1 hour.

Knock back the dough by squashing with your fist and divide into 20 even-sized pieces – keep covered with a clean tea towel so they don't dry out. Shape each one into a sausage and place on an oiled baking tray. Cover with oiled plastic wrap and leave to rise for about 1 hour until doubled in size again.

Preheat the oven to 200°C (400°F).

Remove the plastic wrap and cook the buns on the top shelf for 8–10 minutes, until golden. Cool on a wire rack.

To decorate, mix the icing sugar with a little water until stiff but spreadable, adding food colouring, if you like. Dip in the top of each bun and scatter with sprinkles.

MONKEY FACES

MAKES 16 BISCUITS

Jam biscuits, which are particularly delicious slightly stale.

INGREDIENTS

100 g (⅓ cup) unsalted butter, softened
175 g (generous ¾ cup) caster sugar,
   plus extra for sprinkling
1 large egg
1 tsp vanilla paste
200 g (1⅓ cups) plain flour
370 g (13 oz) jar of strawberry jam

EQUIPMENT

Smiley face and round cookie cutters

METHOD

To make the biscuits, mix together the butter and sugar in a bowl with a wooden spoon until well combined. Add the egg and vanilla and continue to beat by hand until fully incorporated. You will need to scrape the edges of the bowl down for this part.

Tip the flour into the mixture and fold together until fully combined, then shape into a ball. Roll the dough out onto a floured sheet of baking parchment to a depth of around 5 mm (¼ inch). Transfer the sheet to a baking tray and put in the fridge for 10 minutes to firm up.

Remove from the fridge and using a smiley face cookie cutter, take half the dough and cut out 16 shapes. With the other half, just cut out 16 rounds of the same size to act as the bases for the biscuits. Return to the fridge.

Recombine your dough off-cuts and reroll them on a floured surface. Try to be fairly quick doing this as the mixture will warm up and get sticky. If it does, just pop it back in the fridge to firm up again before cutting out more biscuits.

Once the shapes are cut out, arrange on two baking sheets lined with baking parchment and leave to cool in the fridge for 10 mins.

Preheat the oven to 190°C (375°F). Bake the biscuits for 7 minutes, then take them out of the oven and sprinkle the tops with caster sugar. Return all the biscuits to the oven and cook for a further 5 minutes. Take out and allow to cool fully on a wire rack.

When the biscuits are cool, spread jam on the bottom biscuits and top with the face biscuits, sandwiching them together. These will keep for 2–3 days in an airtight container.

LAMINGTONS

MAKES 12 LAMINGTONS

INGREDIENTS

180 g (¾ cup) softened salted butter
185 g (generous ¾ cup) caster sugar
2 tsp vanilla extract
3 eggs
280 g (scant 2 cups) self-raising flour
Pinch of sea salt
140 ml (generous ½ cup) milk
Desiccated coconut, for decorating
500 g (1½ cups) raspberry jam, for decorating

CHOCOLATE ICING

500 g (4 cups) icing (confectioners') sugar
4 tbsp cocoa powder
4–6 tbsp boiling water
½ tsp salted butter
Few drops of vanilla extract

METHOD

Preheat the oven to 180°C (350°F). Grease a 30 x 20 cm (12 x 8 inch) lamington tin and line the base with baking parchment.

Using an electric mixer (or if your kids are nearby use their muscles and a whisk), cream the butter, then gradually beat in the sugar with the vanilla until the mixture is light and fluffy. Gradually beat in the lightly beaten eggs or, if using a mixer, add the eggs one at a time and beat well after each addition.

Sift the flour and salt and then fold into the creamed mixture alternately with the milk, beginning and ending with flour. Add a little more milk if necessary so that the mixture drops easily from the spoon.

Spread the mixture evenly in the tin and bake for 30–35 minutes or until cooked. Cool on a wire rack, then cut into small oblong shapes or cubes.

For the chocolate icing, sift the icing sugar and cocoa into a bowl. Add the boiling water, butter and vanilla, then stir until smooth and shiny.

Spread some of the desiccated coconut on a large plate. Spread the jam onto the cake shapes quite liberally, then place in the fridge for 15 minutes. Dip the cake shapes into the chocolate icing, then immediately roll in the coconut. Leave on a wire rack, in the fridge, to set.

NOT A PAID

Service

ANNOUNCEMENT

BY NIKKI FRIEDLI,
SPIRIT ANIMAL, FLOOR WIZARD

Who experiences more stress than a surgeon*, receives secondary recognition, and is constantly asked if they have a real job? Yes, it's a waiter!

It doesn't matter how long you've worked as a waiter, someone will inevitably throw out a casual, 'So, what're you studying?' The first 1000 times I was asked, my irritation was palpable. There would be a 30-second pause where I mustered all my physical energy into not rolling my eyes so hard I could see into the future. It took a 1001 asks for my indignation to morph into curiosity, for me to hear the question differently – why would I opt for a lifetime of playing second fiddle?

For a long while, I put the question down to my age and being a woman. My obvious owning of my female reproductive system. But not my tits … guys love my tits. They do matter, but there is a much larger, overarching factor in play that encompasses those two factors quite neatly and which involves lots of words that get people all riled up. In terms of visible representation and population, Australia is mostly a – deep breath, the trigger words are coming – white, male-centric culture that does not easily lend itself to conceptualising a career based entirely around giving.

Service is perceived as something you provide when you have no other choice, when your back is against the wall. You're indentured to this way of life because you're either on your way to somewhere else or you deserve to be at the bottom rung, providing a back to step on for others on their way up.

People are genuinely baffled that that you could want to dedicate a career to being tossed in the whims of hundreds of people a night. To be honest, there are nights where I wonder why, why, why, GOD WHY am I here? Generally it involves having smiled through my teeth at a man named 'Kimbo' who just wants to know why there isn't 'an honest bloody Shiraz for me and Maaaarlborough Savvy B for the missus' on the list. Or it's my fourth gluten-free who has really twisted my flaps over how gluten-free everything is, but then eats her friend's cake for dessert while flashing me what she presumes is a laissez-faire wink of delight. It's not; it's a lazy-eyed attempt to prevent her shame from spilling onto the floor so I can wear it as a victory scarf.

*That's an actual thing. Google it.

It's incomprehensible in a society where we're taught from a young age, directly or indirectly, that serving yourself is the key to happiness. Your joy will be built around you and then flow outwards from there. Operating inversely, where we build for others to power ourselves, has an air of perverse backwards-ness. It's ingrained in us that it's naive and unhealthy to operate with the aim of bringing satisfaction to others. Constantly exhausting yourself to exclusively please others is debilitating, fruitless and dangerous. However, sharing a pleasure with someone in accordance with your own limits, in a space that you've created for your own and their enjoyment, is magical.

When you dive headfirst into this career and the restaurant stops being a building and instead becomes an extension of you, you cease being a singular organism. Instead you become integrated into a complex machine that's capable of producing something everyone has chased since we crawled out from the swamp: happiness. Or at least 5 minutes of symphonic distraction without the void of fear niggling away at you daily. By being willing to serve something bigger than yourself, you get to become something bigger than yourself, and there's something pretty freeing about that.

The reality is that what we do scares people. There's vulnerability in exposing just a little hint of what lives inside of you. Sure, everyone has a 'service' persona, but there's a strand of a core that we'll tie from you to us. As a waiter, you let someone crawl into your brain for a few hours and snap at your synapses. That warmth you get when a restaurant engulfs you is the feeling of a team of people unstitching themselves and swallowing you whole. Our job is to be human and that is a shit of a CV to fill.

What I'm really saying is that if your kid doesn't go to uni and become an insufferable engineer or lawyer, they can be a waiter or a stripper. I can tell you that the latter definitely have all the integrity and community any person could need. For once, that's not sarcasm. Being a waiter is about 30 seconds away from being a sex worker, but with shittier tips and an uglier uniform. No shame in being in the pleasure game.

Look, that's probably enough emotions (which are disgusting) for today, so let's drop some bombs about how to host a killer dinner party in your own home. To nail that authentic hospitality feel, we've got a few tips to truly add a little service magic to your night and let you live the front-of-house dream.

1.

Invite 130 people to your home to give them a night you've invested your life experience in and want to share with people so they can dabble in affordable escapism for an evening.

2.

Make it clear that you have to wrap it up at midnight to be mindful of the neighbours. Spend 30 minutes with each person politely justifying this and asking them to leave, please, for the love of God.

3.

Spend hours arranging everything to be at peak functionality balanced with visual appeal. Watch all of them move your furniture and set up without asking and complain that the temperature everywhere is simultaneously too hot and too cold, and that all of the music is simultaneously too loud and too soft.

4.

Cater to their dietaries even though you asked them about 20,000 times before they arrived if they had any. Good luck finding anything in your kitchen that doesn't have a shadow and has only faced due south over the solstice.

5.

DON'T succumb to the urge to strangle Andy (32, man-bun, loves yoga retreats, is 'absolutely an ally to women') who has used the sentence 'I don't mean to be a hassle, but ...' before grilling you on how he doesn't think anything is coeliac-friendly while drinking a beer.

6.

Offer a great selection of wines. Listen to people complain loudly that there isn't enough wine from an obscure region of Mauritius they visited once on holiday with their third wife.

7.

Provide six different kinds of beer. Receive lecture from Dave (28, sleeve tattoos, graphic designer sometimes, ironic beard, LOVES *Black Mirror*) about how none of these are TRULY micro-breweries and he just really thinks this experience would be heightened by a triple-hopped, raspberry-licked, oatmeal-bathed, Pope-blessed IPA from Things White People Like Breweries.

8.

Spend the entire evening avoiding ANY and ALL discussion about 'What technically constitutes a natural wine'.

9.

A SOMMELIER IN ATTENDANCE TALKING ABOUT EVERY WINE: 'This wine is faulty. You know, when I was in the Jura ...'

10.

Explain repeatedly over the course of the night that the ceviche is meant to be raw.

11.

Watch everyone leave.

12.

Lie down. Try not to cry. Cry a lot.

IF NOT, WINE NOT

Hooch, Shots and Bowls

BECAUSE THERE ARE SO MANY RIDICULOUS NAMES FOR COCKTAILS, WE DECIDED TO USE THE MOST ABSURD, WITH THE HELP OF ONE OF OUR BIGGEST INSPIRATIONS: MONTY PYTHON. MOST OF THE NAMES HERE WERE ACTUALLY WHAT *THE FLYING CIRCUS* WAS GOING TO BE CALLED BEFORE THEY SETTLED ON THE NAME WE KNOW AND LOVE.

BUN, WHACKETT, BUZZARD, STUBBLE AND BOOT

MAKES 1

Modern life is so demanding, who actually has time to cook for a dinner party anymore? This four-course meal of shots is great for weight loss, longevity, anti-ageing and fighting with your racist relatives. Or just with yourself, alone in the dark eating two-minute noodles and watching the same three crime shows on Netflix.

INGREDIENTS

30 ml (1 fl oz) Campari
30 ml (1 fl oz) vodka
30 ml (1 fl oz) tequila
30 ml (1 fl oz) whisky
30 ml (1 fl oz) Snachiatto – 15 ml (½ fl oz milk and 15 ml (½ fl oz) Patrón XO Cafe

METHOD

Shoot in order for the full-meal effect.
Or put it all in one cup if it's been a really apocalyptic week.

HANDLEBAR MOUSTACHE HUZZAH

MAKES 1

It's a negroni with olives. Salty, wrong, right – so, so right. Proof that you should brine everything, including your resentment for people. The longer you let it marinate in that salt, the better it gets. It's science!

INGREDIENTS

30 ml (1 fl oz) Campari
30 ml (1 fl oz) gin
30 ml (1 fl oz) rosso vermouth
15 ml (½ fl oz) olive brine
Olives, to garnish

METHOD

You can pre-batch this! Yes, yes, yes you can! Treat the mls as 'parts' and it can be in your fridge for whenever. Add ice, stir, sip, close eyes, exhale loudly through nose. Take it to the office in a sippy cup. Your breath will smell like you've eaten a club sandwich. Everyone will be jealous of your lunch.

DRIPPING PICKLEBACK

MAKES 2

Chicken drippings can only be described as gold dust because they're that precious. We hack the drippings by adding some acid, chilli and a splash of bourbon. It's pretty pornographic.

INGREDIENTS

1 roasted chicken, resting juices reserved
    (should be about 3 tbsp)
1 tsp Peri peri sauce (see page 20)
Juice of 1 lemon
1 shot of bourbon

METHOD

Mix everything together, pour into shot glass, throw it back.

It's equally exciting and uncomfortable, like the first time climbing the rope in gym class.

VASELINE PARADE (WHEN YOU NEED TO LUBE UP QUICKLY)

MAKES 1

Are you tired of buying lip balms and never finishing them? Now you can! Use forgotten lip balm in an obnoxious flavour from your handbag or just Carmex if you're poor.

INGREDIENTS

Sichuan pepper, salt and MSG, for rimming
60 ml (2 fl oz) tequila
30 ml (1 fl oz) Cointreau
15 ml (½ fl oz) lime juice
Sugar syrup (if you need it)
Ice

METHOD

Rim your glasses with your forgotten lip balm.

Dip them in your salty Sichuan flavour enhancer.

Put all the other ingredients in a protein shaker (you know, the one you bought when you took those 'before' photos). Top up with ice.

SHAKE SHAKE SHAKE.

Pop the lid of the protein shaker and pour into glasses.

Voilà, as they say in France.

Just like the Handlebar Moustache Huzzah, this recipe can be kept in the fridge. Just remember that fresh citrus doesn't hold, so blend your alcohol and sugar and add your citrus when you're ready to shake. It can also be done as a punch and works great poured over ice with pre-rimmed or DIY rim glasses ready-to-go, which people can then fill themselves.

THE HORRIBLE EARNEST MEGAPODE

SERVES 4

Revitalise the halcyon youth of Passion Pop! Make a punch. If you're an 'adult' now; you can substitute the Passion Pop for Cristal or a rare vintage of Pol Roger. When you're asking for tips, make sure you tell the sommelier you're going to put it in a used milk bottle with kiwi fruits and brandy. Remember how honest and loving you were after your fourth round of Goon of Fortune? Reclaim that.

INGREDIENTS

1 bottle of your preferred sparkling wine
250 ml (9 fl oz) cinnamon sugar syrup (1 part water, 1 part sugar, 2 cinnamon sticks)
A few handfuls of chopped fruits of your liking (or leave them whole – it's your fucking party)
2 litres (70 fl oz) of your favourite flavour of juice

METHOD

Pour everything into a large bowl.

Put another big bowl of ice right next to it (don't put it in – nobody likes punch that tastes like global warming).

Fill a cup with ice.

Fill the cup with Horrible Earnest Megapode.

Have teary conversation with Greg in the bathroom about how he should leave Sharon. He's worth so much more.

Man hugs.

MIKE BENNIE'S EXETER DAIQUIRI

MAKES 1 JUG

One of the Australian hospitality community's most authentic and favourite bars is found in the belly of Adelaide's blessed Exeter Hotel pub. Many a long drinking session has occurred on this hallowed turf, often resulting in unique and culturally shifting ideas emerging. One such day (or night) saw the gestation and birth of one of the most revered and yet rarely seen 'cocktails', the utterly potent and readily sharable Exeter Daiquiri.

METHOD

Pour 1 bottle of cold 'house white wine' into a jug filled with ice.

Pour a single glass of 'house rosé wine' into the white wine and 1 glass of red wine, preferably out of a foil bag.

Add 3 (or 4) 30 ml (1 fl oz) shots of good, dry gin.

Garnish with lemon and lime pieces, squeezed into the jug. Stir roughly. Pour with gusto into small beer glasses or tumblers.

MICHELADA

★ ★ ★

SERVES 1 PERSON ON A HOT DAY

The best thing about Mexico isn't the food, the mezcal, the people, the weather, the cheap cocaine or Paris nightclub in Tijuana ... it's the micheladas. The Bloody Mary of beer.

INGREDIENTS

1 litre (35 fl oz) bottle of chilled tomato
    juice
3 bottles of chilled pilsner
125 ml (½ cup) lime juice
1 ½ tsp Worcestershire sauce
1 tsp hot sauce
1 tsp Maggi seasoning

2 tbsp sea salt
½ tsp chilli powder
Chillies and lime wedges, to serve

METHOD

Mix the tomato juice, beer, lime juice, Worcestershire sauce, hot sauce and Maggi seasoning together in a large jug.

Mix the salt and chilli powder together on a small plate. Rub the rims of tall glasses with the lime wedges and dip in the salt mixture.

Fill the glasses with ice, add the Michelada mixture and garnish with chillies and more lime wedges.

HOW TO RUN A KITCHEN ON PASSIVE AGGRESSIVE POST IT NOTES

DUNCAN WELGEMOED

I'd like to thank everyone that has ever supported us. Thank you to all our customers, suppliers and producers that continually support our weird vision.

Special thanks to my mum Gail and dad Peter (for everything, truly), Cath (for putting up with my shit for more than a decade; this ain't a star, but it's close), Suse and the Hazels. My South African family, especially Barbie, Anne, Lee, Corrie and the cousins. The Glendinnings, Brian especially.

My beautiful bouncing boys – Alexander William Ralph and Maxwell Robert Glendinning. One day I hope you read this book and forgive the language.

Our partners in crime: JB, Pricey and Loz.

Our weapon Head chef Imogen, who helped make this book and keep Africola running. I am lucky to know you and I hope we will be cooking together for a very long time. All our staff past and present, Lozza, Cam, Prim, Joel, Hugh dog, Romy, Mama Jen, Courtney, Kate, Baby Stef, Big Stef, Rosie, Brooke

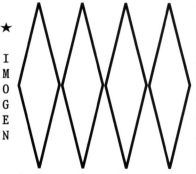

I
M
O
G
E
N

★

Sophie, Coco, I love you all so much! Except the ones we fired, y'all are banned. Friedli pants for the words and the work, meme lord and service queen. Muchas Gracias.

Special thanks to James Hillier. Without your belief, hard work and dedication, none of this would be possible. Sondra Hillier for being the best and making sure the businesses function. I will get around to scanning those receipts one day.

SNM for TCB always. My PT Aude Juno, who is the best therapist and most patient person I know. Inspector Rimington – stronger than granite and the real apex predator.

Our friends: AG, Brian, Varuni, The Femmes, Burgo, M North and Imogen Young, Moyle, Morgs, Victor, Paulie, Taras, Amber, Jauma, BK and Fam, Gaz Dog Belton and Rainbo, Mickey D, Mike Patton, Bill Bailey, Driely S, Kev the Legend, Big Dog Matheson, Myffy

Rigby (thanks for the edits), Max V, Manu, Pete, Matty Orlando, Jimmy Spreds, Reggie, Norbert, Rough Rice, Koral, Tom and fam, Jason Stephenson, Henk Kruger, John King, Prim, Mona crew, Mike Bennie, Nick Stock, Tamrah P (love you babes), Clem Fjord, Em Davis, The real Jason Isaacs, Orlando Bloom, Sharon Romeo, Whitey!!, Diplo, Pussy Riot, Monty, Rob, Poes Lusted, JP, NIN and Trent, SATC, my brothers and sisters, aunties and uncles in Yirrkala, Johan and Kate, Pat, Lennox, Maria Taka, Niki Nakazawa Pynto, Oz Harvest, Starlight Charity, Many Faces of Cancer, Still Aware, Troy, the Mcconnell brothers, Holly and The Lucas Group, Karlien, Candice Keller, Ben Cooper, D Lomardo, The Chad, Zai, The Bear Koffman, Nanny, Clayton and Tanya, Brendan Unico, Flea, Eddie Izzard, Juzzy Lane, Footie, Bad news Sam Hughes (RIP), Pippa (RIP), #PaulCarmicheal, Elvis and Ben, the Loves, Muircroft, C Boys, Lee tran, Wazza, MJK, Mary's Group, Forte bro's, St. John restaurant, The Nut Tree, Chris Manfield and Margie, The Shulkins Scampi and the Camps, Biggles, Worlds Apart Wine, Meira and Banjo, my Mexican families, Kenny and Jakey boy (love you bastards), The Happy Motel, Ross Ganf, Marilyn Manson and the hundreds of dear friends that are so close to my heart and too many to mention.

Corinne, Mr Wolfers, and the whole Murdoch Books crew, your patience has been appreciated.

And my mentor MPW, my dear friend, thank you for everything you do for me.

And to all the haters – fok julle naaiers. We won't believe in the things that won't believe in us.

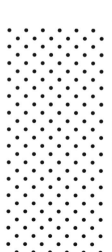

JAMES BROWN

Thank you to all and everyone who has supported this funky organism.

To the stolen land of the Kaurna People that gives us all our sustenance. We pay our respects to the Kaurna people from elders to youngsters, past, present and emerging. Big respect to Jamie Goldsmith.

All the current staff and all those who have moved on elsewhere, so many legends back and front of house. From staff member #1 Nantale (my only hire)! Thank you to all of you for allowing me to dip my grubby mitts in the staffy pot! Nikki for the last minute bookings and Mo especially for the late night feeds. And the suppliers, subcontractors like Nida our darling cleaner! And to Prim my brother from another Burundi Mama, I can hear your Tony Abbott bullshit and laughter from level 3!

P
R
I
M

The special people who make it all possible, the extended fam. Honey Mama Nicole Tamagotchi Donnelly aka McGirlver and angel baby Olive Pink Do-Da-Donnelly-Brown, Alex and Angie Donnelly you guys are the best, Chef Mama Lesley, Papa James Brown VII. Clare, David, Dr. Drae and Cashy. Auntie Sexy Kazbah to! Love you all.

To the Smock Bureau art posse who helped make the place, from version 1-2. Kaspar Schmidt Mumm, Anal Andy Irwin, Lucas Croall Bags, Private Meatball Gab Cole, Gerry Wedd and Karlien Vispoes Van Rooyen. To all my old crews for your helpings, UFO (RIP), Mash Baby Beers Chicken Sanga Crew. Clairo Saswick-Smith, Seb Sweb (IOU a few), PapaDom Roberts; 5 O'clock Pat, Sassy Selena, Lil' Biscuit, Normal Person's Conditioner Cuttlefish. The whole OMG Crew Tom Smokey Robbo, Naomi big love above to Ajier :((RIP brother). Ballen, Keita, Samba, Lasker and most importantly SuperBejo and your posse!

Book team: ultimate wunderkind Emmaline Zannelli, Simon "Beez" Bajada

switch king and king offender of the Re-use Police, Anthony "Ant God" Gagliardi Business Man.

To Corinne, Megan, Justin at Murdoch Books, it has been a real pleasure working with each of you.

Special mention and thanks to Adrian "Consigliere" Tisato, Sam Weckert, Surahn & Pussy Sosij and Amber, Driely Carter, Niki Nakazawa and Maria Itaka and Maeve O'meara.

To the partners Paul Trigger-It Glen, Nikki, Pricey and DW aka Papa Fucking Milko and to the skateboarding accident-compound-fracture that lead to this Cassius Clay chaotic train ride.

Finally, all our lies have come true!

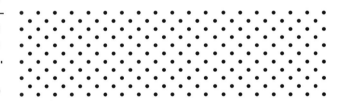

D
W

J
B

INDEX

★ ★ ★

Published in 2020 by Murdoch Books,
an imprint of Allen & Unwin

Murdoch Books Australia
83 Alexander Street
Crows Nest NSW 2065
Phone: +61 (0)2 8425 0100
murdochbooks.com.au
info@murdochbooks.com.au

Murdoch Books UK
Ormond House
26-27 Boswell Street
London WC1N 3JZ
Phone: +44 (0) 20 8785 5995
murdochbooks.co.uk
info@murdochbooks.co.uk

For corporate orders and
custom publishing, contact
our business development team at
salesenquiries@murdochbooks.com.au

Publisher: Corinne Roberts
Editorial Manager: Justin Wolfers
Design Manager: Megan Pigott
Editor: Kay Delves
Creative/Art Director: James Brown
Graphic Designer: Anthony Gagliardi
Graphic Design Assistant: Tyrone Ormsby
Custom Typeface Design: Business Fonts
Food Photographer: Simon Bajada
Food Stylist: James Brown/Simon Bajada
Art Photographer: Emmaline Zanelli
Art Stylist: Emmaline Zanelli
Author/Chef: Duncan Welgemoed
Food Assistant: Imogen Czulowski
Writing Contribution: Nikki Friedli
Prop Supply: Karen Lewis
Production Director: Lou Playfair

ISBN 978 1 76052 386 2 Australia
ISBN 978 1 76063 464 3 UK

A catalogue record for this
book is available from the
National Library of Australia

Colour reproduction by Splitting Image
Colour Studio Pty Ltd, Clayton, Victoria
Printed by Hang Tai Printing Company
Limited, China

TABLESPOON MEASURES: We have used 20 ml
(4 teaspoon) tablespoon measures. If you
are using a 15 ml (3 teaspoon) tablespoon
add an extra teaspoon of the ingredient
for each tablespoon specified.

10 9 8 7 6 5 4 3 2 1

South African by birth, Duncan was head chef at The Goose at Britwell Salome, Watlington, Oxford when it was awarded a Michelin star in 2005 and has also worked at Le Manoir aux Quat'Saisons. In early 2010, he arrived in South Australia and opened Africola in 2014. Over the years, Duncan has become Adelaide's (un)official spirit animal — mythical beast, troublemaker, conversation starter. His latest restaurant, Africola, tells a story close to his heart. It has since been awarded 4.5/5 Australians by The Australian's food editor John Lethlean, featured in countless magazines, newspapers and TV shows around the world and frequented by rockstars and celebrities alike. Business partner, James Brown, runs a design agency and has designed the interiors of Africola and many iconic venues including Hong Kong's Happy Paradise, Bali's Motel Mexicola (the most instagrammed hotel in the world) and Melbourne's Hotel Jesus. Together, they are a formidable creative force.